Where's the Minestrone?

An Italian American Explores Italy

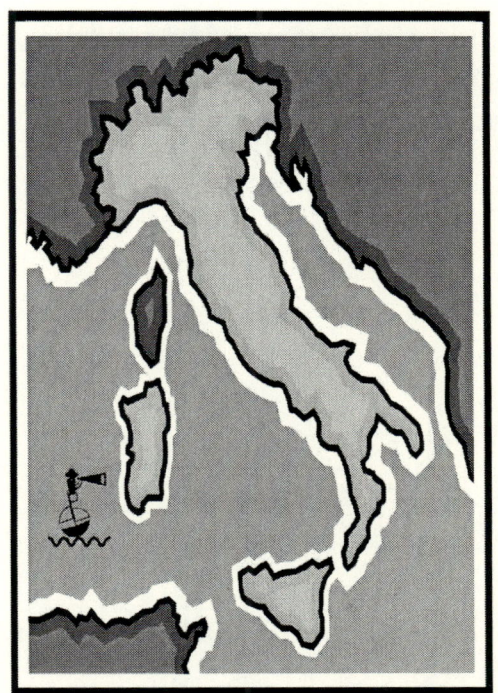

Peter Carusone

Copyright © 2006 by Peter Carusone

ISBN-13: 978-1-4116-0027-0
ISBN-10: 978-1-4116-0027-0

First printing 2006

All rights reserved, including the right of reproduction in whole or in part in any form, except by reviewers who may quote brief excerpts in connection with a review.

Printed in the United States of America.

Peter Carusone
peter.carusone@wright.edu
http://www.lulu.com/PeterCarusone

Dedication

To the memory of my father, Gennaro "Geno the Great" Carusone (June 26, 1918 – December 2, 1999), whose love of family shaped our values and earned our deepest respect.

To Gloria Carusone, my wife, always a wise and supportive friend, a delightful companion ever optimistic, full of life and inspiring.

To my wonderful children, Nancy, Geno, Steve, Tom and Tony, their spouses, and the many wonderful grandchildren they have given me.

To the memory of my grandfather, Pietro Carusone (December 26, 1879 – September 3, 1955) without whose foresight and adventurous spirit none of us would be here in this wonderful land of the free.

Acknowledgements

Appreciation and kudos to the many friends and acquaintances who helped me learn what I needed to know about the language and the culture, and who provided invaluable resources to facilitate my travels to *Bel Italia* and my work on this book.

This includes Bruno Greco, Rory Golden, Terry and Caroline McConville, Jorge Rodriguez, Jera Pecotte, Lorenzo Ferraro, Bob and Lorraine Wagley, Jim and Janice Kremer, Tom Dovel, the family proprietors of Noe's Pizzeria in Torino, and many others. Those who shared professional expertise and useful critiques at various stages of manuscript development include Jayne Raparelli, Phil Paradis, Joanne Glenn, Greg Banks, Gloria (my wife), Geno (my son), Mark, and many of my students.

Special thanks and recognition to Mark Judd for his encouragement and his help in supplying material relevant to the book. Mark was a great sounding board and a source of first hand knowledge of how the Italian system works, and doesn't work.

Contents

PART I: Antipasti

Chapter	1	Theme	1
Chapter	2	Glimpses	7
Chapter	3	Reflections	13
Chapter	4	Cheers	25
Chapter	5	That's Italian!	37

PART II: Primi Piatti

Chapter	6	Arrival	47
Chapter	7	*Il professore*	59
Chapter	8	Where's the Minestrone?	75
Chapter	9	*Non c'e' male*	91
Chapter	10	What's Your Hand Doing In My Pocket?	107

PART III: Secondi Piatti

Chapter	11	Connection	123
Chapter	12	Don You Toucha Da Banana!	135
Chapter	13	What! You Don't Like the Food?!!	151

PART IV: Contorni

Chapter	14	Bureaucracy Italian Style	167
Chapter	15	*Buon compleanno!*	183
Chapter	16	Rome	201
Chapter	17	*Magna Italia*	213

PART V: Dolce

Chapter	18	Meatballs, Mischief & Miscellany	223
Chapter	19	Welcome to America	233
Chapter	20	Wah, I Miss It and Wanna Go Back!	243

| Epilogue | About the Book | 259 |
| Appendix | Noe's Menu | 261 |

A note about the transcripts of original correspondence, emails and other personal notes: When including the text of any official or personal written material, the author retained the original spelling, capitalization, grammar and punctuation throughout this book although it may include errors. Rather than call undue attention to errors by Italians using their 'best' English, and vice-versa, the author has instead elected to waive the use of the conventional [sic] notation in order to preserve the authenticity and flow of the dialogues.

The astute reader will notice not only some less than perfect translations by Italian speakers of their ideas into English but many more incorrect translations by American speakers of ideas into Italian. This was especially true on the part of the author who on so many occasions succeeded in wholesale butchering of the world's most beautiful and melodic language.

Disclaimer: With reference to comments attributed to others, in each case efforts have been made to verify the accuracy of said statements, often with the aid of supporting documentation, and often to disguise or eliminate quoted comments that could be embarrassing to the person whose words were cited. Of course, the author apologizes for any errors or lapses in judgment that may have occurred or inadvertently slipped through.

1

THEME

The opportunity of a lifetime. A chance to see the land my grandparents left behind nearly 70 years ago.

This is a book about Italy. There are several reasons why you might be interested in reading such a book:

(a) You are Italian.
(b) You think it would be fun to be Italian.
(c) You have studied about Italy for many years and want to know more.
(d) You have actually been to Italy but still do not have the foggiest notion of what is really going on over there.

If you fall into the latter category, not to worry. There are people who have spent a lifetime in Italy and never quite figured it out!

It was during my first visit to the land of Verdi and Garibaldi that I decided to write this book. I was there for

108 days. It was my first such trip and hopefully would not be the last.

At the rather mature age of 56, I was embarking upon my very first voyage outside the North American continent. As an Italian-American, i.e., an American of Italian descent, I had frequently entertained thoughts of someday visiting the country of my family origins.

Friends and relatives often would ask "Pete, you've never been to Italy?" like there was something wrong with me. Well, ever since I could remember, there was always so much to see here in the USA that any thoughts of taking a trip to Europe were not a serious consideration.

Notice if you will, my usage of the term *USA* which, from a European perspective, tends to be more acceptable than simply *U.S.* I first discovered this on a train to Milan when the conductor made known to me his displeasure with the *U.S.* notation preprinted on my Eurailpass, prompting him to inquire rather authoritatively and instructively as to *which* united states I might be coming from!

The look on his face was one of feigned puzzlement and, at the same time, smug satisfaction. He was perturbed as well about the manner in which I had recorded the numbers for that day's date on my pass, which at the time I thought was very picky of him, later realizing that there was good reason for his concern. But more about that later.

My object in writing this book is to share my most vivid experiences during those 108 days, especially from the viewpoint of an Italian-American, one who shares all the experiences, attitudes, and expectations that are fairly common among those raised in an American family with Italian roots. An American first, certainly. But, at the same time, an American who is very proud of my unique heritage and ancestry.

The accomplishments of famous Italians are legion, of course. Michelangelo. Christopher Columbus. Pavarotti. Verdi. Frank Sinatra. Joe Dimaggio. Sophia Loren. Yes,

Italians, and Italian-Americans alike, tend to be quite ethnocentric.

Impressions while growing up still linger. *Everything Italian is the best!* Enough to make a small child wonder... *can it be?* Italian weddings. The music. The dancing. The fun and celebration! Pasta. Pizza. So much to be proud of. But always an American first. And when they greet you in Italy... "Ah, Americano?" "Si, si..." And then to explain that I am *Italo*-Americano, born and raised in Cincinnati, Ohio, my mother born in America, her parents came from Sicily. And *mi padre*? Dad's family was from a small town north of Naples--he was 10 years old in 1928 when the Carusone *familia* migrated.

So, here I sit, 75 years later, savoring the photos, videos, notes, and memories, trying to reconstruct and make sense of it all. Why was I taking this trip anyway? My excuse for going there was to teach. With the support of my good colleagues and friends at Wright State University where I was professor of marketing, I was able to obtain an appointment as visiting professor at the Business School (SAA) of the University of Turin (*Torino*). The chairman of my department made a big deal of it, posting notices like the one below all over the College of Business prior to my departure.

Both Wright State and the University of Torino belong to a worldwide consortium of schools that promotes and facilitates such exchanges, student and faculty alike. In fact, most of the students I taught while in Italy were Americans studying abroad, the rest Europeans. Yes, the courses were taught in English.

That was one of the really neat things about the assignment, the opportunity to work with a small number of students from different countries and really get to know them. All of us working together trying to learn the

> **DR. PETER S. CARUSONE**
>
> has been selected
> to participate in the
>
> **TURIN PROGRAM of the
> UNIVERSITY STUDIES ABROAD CONSORTIUM**
>
> **Fall Semester**
>
> As a faculty member of USAC, Dr. Carusone will be teaching courses in Product Development and Principles of Marketing at the Scuola di Amministrazione Aziendale (SAA) of the University of Turin in Torino, Italy. Dr. Carusone has designed special research projects, which will involve the students with local (Italian) products and stores. There will be a field trip to the Italian Riviera. Although the courses will be taught in English, Dr. Carusone is brushing up on his Italian in preparation for the trip so that he will know how to order pizza, pasta, and risotto.
>
> August 31 - Departure from United States
> December 9 - End of Final Exams
>
> **Buon Viaggio!**

language of our host country, trying to deal with various aspects of culture shock, helping one another and sharing experiences. Like the American students who related their astonishment at fan behavior at a football (soccer) game. And the remarkable contrast between the four female students from Finland, shy and lacking in Italian or English language skills, and the four guys from Denmark, outgoing and boisterous partiers whose command of English was quite good.

In writing this book, I am hoping to provide an enjoyable panorama of glimpses and reflections of those unforgettable experiences, so that the reader might be able to see what I saw and feel what I felt when I was there in *Italia*.

Now, I know this is not entirely possible because it's like trying to capture on film something that is bigger than life. Like driving out West through one of those great states of the United States of America, up a hill and over the rise when all of a sudden the horizon opens up, spanning from far left to far right, as far as the eye can see--breathtaking in its beauty--and then you realize that you cannot possibly take a picture of it, not even with a panoramic lens. You cannot capture it. All you can do is enjoy it! And later try to convey a verbal portrait of the visual sensation.

Here, then, is what I'd like to share with you in this book:

- My experience with the food, the shops, the bars and restaurants, the people and their habitat, driving and other forms of recreational violence, the gypsies, and problems with everyday things.
- What I heard and learned about what others, Italians and Americans alike, including the American and European students at the school thought.
- A critical look at popular beliefs about Italy and about Italian food. Did you know that *Italian* food is vastly different from *Italian-American* fare? I didn't. And where did meatballs come from? Who invented pizza anyway?
- My constant search for signs of connection between Italian and Italian-American, always

exploring the similarities and differences, looking for things that my grandfather might have recognized were he still alive.
- My disappointment and frustration in trying to fulfill the sentimental part of my journey: the search for those elusive Carusone family roots.
- Occasional bewilderment and emotional turmoil in trying to deal with important family issues from back home, continents and thousands of miles away.
- My joy and happiness at being able to share in the Italian passion for life, participate in conversation in that beautiful and melodic language, sensing a kind of unspoken kinship beneath it all.

In short, things "over there" are quite different from what they seem to be from here. From what we have read and heard about Italy. From what we have been taught and what we would expect to find. From what we thought it meant to be *Italian*!

Looking at the Table of Contents, the reader will notice that the organization of the book follows closely the format of a typical Italian menu. Enjoy! Or as my Aunt Rose used to say, *Mangia!*

Part I	Antipasti	Appetizer
Part II	Primi Piatti	First Course
Part III	Secondi Piatti	Second Course
Part IV	Contorni	Side Dishes
Part V	Dolce	Dessert

2

GLIMPSES

Italy is a land of many faces that are bewildering when viewed through the eyes of *lo straniero* (the foreigner).

Before, during, and after the trip, I digested hundreds of news articles about life in Italy, Italian culture and customs, current events, and Italian food. Here are a few of those items, especially ones that influenced my early expectations and later interpretations of the Italian scene.

· · ·

> There are two foods that Italians are willing to be seen eating in the streets: pizza and ice cream. Some other classic street snacks include hot roasted chestnuts, coconut slices, unsalted green olives and salted lupines.

· · ·

> McDonald's aims to double the number of its outlets in Italy.

• • •

Italy and Spain rank highest among EU countries as a place to live by Americans working abroad. Germany and Ireland, by contrast, are ranked relatively low.

• • •

A survey of Italian tourists visiting New York City says the most popular consumer buys are Ray Ban sunglasses, Levi's jeans, and Timberland shoes.

• • •

Roughly the size of California, Italy has a population of 60 million. The number of tourists visiting Italy, mainly from April through August, is 30 million. Most of the tourists come from Germany, France, UK, USA, Austria, and Switzerland.

• • •

The U.S.A. has surpassed Italy as the world's largest pasta consumer. Worried that the U.S.A. might be perfecting the art of pasta, the Italians began furiously trying to catch up by investing in new food technology to develop whole new pasta.

• • •

Shipments of Italian pasta to the U.S. more than doubled during the 1990s. The American pasta industry filed a complaint, arguing that foreign producers were using government subsidies at home to sell pasta in the U.S.A. at prices below cost.

• • •

Nutella, a gooey hazelnut and chocolate spread made in Italy, is one of the world's great junk foods. Nutella may change American ideas about all Italian food being healthier and more natural.

• • •

Eating is banned on Rome's Spanish Steps. The Rome City Council declared that tourists eating food while sitting on the famous Spanish Steps will be breaking the law.

• • •

Italian cities, including Rome, Milan, Naples, and Turin, fight pollution by limiting cars. At least 11 cities impose alternate day driving rules which involve even-numbered plates being permissible one day, odd the next, when pollution is too high.

• • •

Italian police crack down on purse snatchings and other crimes against tourists.

• • •

Travel scams: A tourist describes how she and her husband were robbed at the airport in Turin, Italy, by thieves who poured chocolate goop on her husband, then offered to help clean it up while quietly emptying the pockets of his jacket.

• • •

A nice little funeral earner comes to haunt Turin. Two Roman Catholic priests in Turin, Italy, were sought in connection with a complex racket involving bribes for tipping off undertakers about deaths of members of their flocks. The priests allegedly took kickbacks for providing lists of local deaths.

. . .

Northern Italy, center of the unification movement of the 19th Century when the regions and city-states came together as a nation, is said to have implemented laws benefiting the regions north of Rome, thereby leaving the South to stagnate while contributing taxes for northern economic expansion.

. . .

Unemployment rates in the south of Italy average two to three times those of the north, and can reach as high as 25 percent.

. . .

Injured British lorry driver refuses to allow Italians to operate. A severely injured truck driver stranded in a hospital in Turin, Italy, turns down an operation because he thinks Italy is an underdeveloped country and he wants a British doctor. The man's family flies to Turin to try to persuade him to change his mind.

. . .

Italians are pioneers in medical science, boasting the first medical school and the first post-mortems of the Western world, and other notable discoveries. For example, it was Gabriele Falloppio in the 16th Century who discovered the tubes that now bear his name; and he invented the condom.

. . .

If you find yourself on the way to an Italian hospital, be sure to stop along the way to buy your own supply of drinking water, a glass, paper napkins, silverware, soap, towels, and toilet paper.

3

REFLECTIONS

It took about a year to get ready for the trip. In retrospect, I don't know how I could have done it without the help and moral support of my large family—my parents, my offspring in two generations, my wife's side of the family, 30 in all—together with a network of friends and acquaintances, many of whom had useful information or contacts and were eager to help. My thoughts were with them during my travels.

To keep in touch I used every form of communication imaginable with the possible exception of smoke signals. There was a steady stream of postcards and letters, telephone calls, faxes and even some email. The postal service was more reliable than I had been led to believe it would be, with delivery time of 10 to 14 days in either direction.

The telephone was faster but outrageously expensive, as my wife and I would discover to our chagrin when the first phone bill arrived. The charges were so high, in fact, that a representative of AT&T contacted Gloria one day asking if our calling card had been lost or stolen. He said their records showed that someone in Italy was billing a lot of international calls to our number. No kidding! Maybe when your bill exceeds $1,000 in one month they get suspicious. I must say it was worth it, however, Gloria and I having celebrated our first wedding anniversary just two weeks prior to my departure from the States and missing each other as newlyweds do.

Prior to the trip, we had planned to use email for cheap daily contact but, due to technology limitations at the time, we were able to use it only sporadically. Big disappointment. So, to keep in touch with the rest of my large and closely-knit family, I would come to rely mainly on the fax for timely communication.

Not that I ever totally gave up on email. I would sit at a computer in Lorenzo's *"laboratorio"* (a large office with about eight computer stations) trying to make a connection every day that I had reason to be at school. Lorenzo was the computer *capo* and guru of the school. He was exceedingly generous in letting me use his computers to try to access my email account.

Trying was the word that kept flashing on the monitor. After five minutes... ten minutes... still *trying*. Trying, incidentally, is something you get used to very quickly on the Italian peninsula. Trying to find a grocery store open on Wednesday afternoons, or a pizzeria that's open on Mondays. Trying to find a cup of coffee on a Sunday morning. Trying to find a way to get around when the buses are on strike, or to find out *why* they're on strike in the first place, as if anybody cared. Trying to send email back home.

So, what was the problem with the Internet and email connection at the university? One day I would be told it had to do with the server at the school. Other days I was led to believe the problem was with the telephone lines, or that in the afternoon it is impossible to get through due to the heavy traffic from the USA, where, due to the six-hour time difference, it would be the beginning of the workday. Surprisingly, no one suggested that the problem might have to do with the full moon!

. . .

Writing and sending faxes to a large number of people, even once a week, could be a laborious and time-consuming task. It could take time away from the opportunity to travel and immerse oneself in the culture of this fascinating country. That is something I definitely wanted to avoid! So, I found a way early on to keep in touch with everyone back home but without having to repeat myself or send everyone a separate communiqué.

It was good talking to you tonight, Geno. Thanks for calling. Tony called me last weekend. Say, do me a favor and make copies of this FAX and send it to your ugly (haha) brothers and sweet, lovely sister for me. This will save me some time and some FAXES, too!

If only they could have been there with me, that would have been wonderful, of course. Gloria would be flying over for the final four weeks of my stay and that was a blessing. But I never stopped wondering, throughout my travels and encounters, just how the kids, my parents and other relatives, even my beloved deceased grandparents, aunts and uncles, would react to the people and places of modern-day Italy. I hoped my messages back home would somehow convey a sense of being there with me as well as provide information about how I was acclimating.

I trust all of you are fine. I know you've been talking with Gloria. Maybe she's told you that I'm really keeping busy with learning "the system." I mean, everything is different in some way or another, including things like how to use the phone, where to buy the little cards (called "gettone") that you often need to use a payphone, what to say when you get an Italian who doesn't know any English, where to buy the bus passes (the buses don't take money), where to catch the bus, how to get on and off (different doors), how to know when to get off (I've messed that up several times since they don't have many street sign— only nameplates on the sides of the corner buildings which, of course, are impossible to see at night!), how to mail a letter, where to buy the stamps, how to get money from the bank, etc, etc.

. . .

The little things like buying the stamps, getting money from the bank, were just that—little things I needed to learn so that I could get around. But I also found perplexing challenges "at home." For example, I'd been told that the washing machine in the apartment was brand new, so I believed it was state of the art. The machine was quite small by our standards, situated along a wall in the narrow bathroom between washbasin and the toilet and bidet. To use it, first you had to reach behind the machine, open the water valve, plug the cord into the electrical outlet on the far side of the sink, remove whatever might be sitting on top of the washer because it is a top-loading machine, pull open the top, loosen the clamp on the side-mounted drum, put in clothes and detergent, close and clamp it shut, drop down the top and, finally, adjust and activate the control knob to desired setting. Lucky for me, the instruction manual was written in Italian and English.

Right now it is noon on Sunday (6:00 a.m. in Ohio) and I am writing on the laptop what I will fax to you tomorrow from school. I am sitting here in my jammies having coffee, cereal, and fruit, waiting for the washing machine to finish a load of sheets so I can hang them up and maybe they will be dry by tonight. I can't take a shower yet because I don't want to turn on the hot water heater while the washer is going in case it would blow a fuse or something.

It is a cute little washer, brand new, very compact and energy efficient. But it takes about two hours to do a small load of laundry and spin cycle the water out so that the clothes are ready to be line-dried (very few Italians own dryers). The washer agitates for 7 seconds, then rests for 7 seconds, then agitates, and so on. Very strange.

Oh...Pass it on: If anyone should send me any mail, if it's larger than a standard letter-size, please address it to me at the school, not at the apartment. OK?

The caveat about not sending oversize mail to the *appartamento* was important because the mailbox, located in the hallway downstairs, was quite small and, if something didn't fit, I was told it would be returned to the main post office across town, leaving a note as to where I would have to pick it up. Since I was relying on public transportation, this was another conundrum I was anxious to avoid as it could take half a day just to plan the logistics of such a trip to retrieve a piece of mail.

The big things you can handle. A lot of little things will drive you crazy!

Got home the other night and retrieved my mail but then couldn't get the key out of the lock! I

> *tried for 20 minutes, then called Giuseppina (the landlady) who came the next day and replaced the lock. Yes, I am doing okay in communicating in Italian but not a lot more than the basic stuff like "Where does one find...?" or "Does this bus stop at...?" or "Give me a draft beer in a large glass."*
>
> *Hmmm...just discovered the washer does not take two hours to do a load. Apparently I must have run that first load thru all three cycles instead of just one of the three (cottons, synthetics, delicates)! Gloria, I need you!!!*

Well, I *thought* Giuseppina replaced the lock because after she stopped by it was working again, but after talking with her later in the week it seems all she did was to pull the key out of the lock, and on the very first try! As for the washer, months later, after Gloria arrived and took command of the laundry, it became abundantly clear that my first assessment was, indeed, correct. The washer really did take two hours to do a small load!

. . .

One of my first encounters with Italian generosity took place in a neighborhood *pasticceria* (pastry shop), as I explained in a message to Gloria:

> *I wrote out some more postcards (cartoline) and then took a walk up on Via Triano, which is a busy street with lots of shops not far from (vicino a) the apartment. One thing that's neat is that although the stores close for a few hours early afternoon, when they reopen most of them don't close again until 8:00 p.m. I stopped and bought some stationery at one shop, then got some more postcards at the tobacco shop.*

> *I walked into a pastry shop to try something that looked good in the window (a cookie shaped like a pretzel loop with honey on it). I asked for "tre" (three)—and the owner scooped up handsful and put them in a bag. I said, "No, no, tre" at which point he understood and said, "Ah, tre pezzi?" He was going to give me three kilos. That's about six pounds! Then, he hands me a half dozen cookies and doesn't let me pay for them!*

The generosity I encountered at the pastry shop did not extend to the behavior I experienced when I took to the roads. One of the true enigmas of Italy, not likely to be resolved in this lifetime, has to do with the duality of the Italian psyche. How is it possible for people who are basically so gentle, respectful, helpful, and friendly to suddenly turn into demonic maniacs when put behind the wheel of a car? I am certain that the same person who gave me those cookies could well be sitting there in his little Fiat Cinquecento (500) eager to target me the minute I dared step off the curb. Or even if I didn't step off the curb!

> *This is a strange place...almost like a foreign country (quite a realization for an Italian-American)!! Italian drivers are the rudest, most obnoxious you could ever imagine. No courtesies whatsoever. Just the opposite! They will go out of their way to pull in front of you or block you off. Steve would go bonkers here! This morning it took our bus three changes of the traffic light to make a left turn thru an intersection because none of the cars would move and it was gridlock. They are stubborn and are constantly honking their horns!*

> *You really have to plan ahead because the stores are almost all closed on Sunday, also from about 1:00 to 4:00 p.m. every day of the week. Then, some stores close on Monday or Wednesday, depending.*
>
> *Mark and his fiancée took a train from downtown on Monday, a one-hour ride to this specialty furniture store, only to find out they were closed!*
>
> *You can only buy cigarettes in stores that are actually called "tobacco stores," and most are closed on Sundays. Tobacco stores also are the best source for postage stamps as the post office runs low on stamps by mid-day!*

Figuring out when places are open and when they are closed is something of an art. You have to work at it everyday and plan ahead, because just when you think you've got it, that's when you find out that the rules are subject to change. To their credit, the Italians usually seem to know. Maybe they are born with this information.

• • •

So this is what my days were like: trying to figure out all this stuff, teach classes, make travel arrangements, send faxes, and place telephone calls. By the end of those long hard days, I would be more than ready to stop on the way home for a beer or a mixed drink. I would usually opt for a beer because it was easier to order. *"Una birra!"* That's all. Or, to be polite about it, *"Una birra, per favore."* Or, for a draught beer, *"Una birra alla spina."*

One day, however, I decided to live on the edge. I was craving a martini, a drink that I believed originated in Italia because the Martini and Rossi Company is located right there in Torino, of all places. And the drink is named after the vermouth of the same name, or so I thought. Surely they would know how to make a martini in the local bars. Wrong!

I stopped in a couple of bars and found that nobody knew anything about how to make a martini. This, in spite of the fact that they all carry Martini and Rossi vermouth AND have gin or vodka right on the shelf. Later in the trip I would have the opportunity to tour the Martini and Rossi distillery and see vermouth coming off the line specially formulated and labeled for the U.S. market. After returning to the States, I would further discover that my original presumption about how the Martini name was derived may have been in error.

According to *The Pocket Bartender's Guide* by a Michael Jackson, the fact that the Martini cocktail made with dry vermouth happens to have the same name as the company that makes the vermouth is a coincidence. He says the cocktail was actually invented by a barman in New York called Martini, and that French vermouth was originally used.

. . .

One message I never had to send home was to say that I had been robbed or assaulted. I'd like to think that my good fortune was due to St. Christopher watching over me. Or perhaps my high level of preparedness and vigilance had paid off. Then again, maybe it was just dumb luck.

I knew of others who were not so lucky. Like some of the American students who succumbed to pickpockets or were conned by gypsies. And Professor Bob, a colleague who taught in Torino the year after I did but made the mistake of bringing his billfold with him. For the billfold it was a one-way trip.

I was aware before leaving the States that the incidence of violent crime in Italy is far less than in America. Petty crime, however, is another story, especially in the tourist areas where there is a high rate of pick pocketing, theft from parked vehicles, and purse snatchings.

The Italians do a pretty good job of protecting their homes and places of business by surrounding themselves with walls, gates, and shutters, much like the fortresses of centuries gone by. The neighborhood dry cleaners, for example, locked their door even during times of the day when the store is open for business.

In retrospect, I must say that I never felt seriously threatened in Italy though I did have a few close calls. Like the guy in Naples posing as a porter at the train station. And the break-in of our luggage in Milan. And the ATM that *took* my money instead of giving it to me! In each of these instances the story has a happy ending.

. . .

So many of the messages I sent home were about the food because that was the one thing in which everyone was interested. Ah, Italian food! Isn't that one of the best things about Italy? But the "Italian" food I ate here was so different than the cooking of my aunts, stepmother, and ex-wife, all of whom nurtured the family recipes handed down by Grandma Mathilde. My lunch at the school cafeteria was often roast turkey and French fries—to which they sometimes add a little parsley and often put them on pizza. One bad meal was an Italian sausage that was the absolute fattiest piece of meat I have ever seen. I even began to sample other cuisines—Japanese one night, Chinese or Mexican the next.

So, how come now the food over there is so different? What could possibly account for this remarkable disparity between Italian food and Italian-American food? The spices? The fresh ingredients? The water?

It is said that Italian-Americans have Americanized the food; that they have adapted it to the American palate.

Sure, that sounds good, but that's the easy answer. The truth is, it doesn't hold water when you think about it.

There is another possibility. Someone changed. Of course, I cannot claim to be an expert on the issue of Italian cuisine, but I can tell you that after spending three-and-one-half months in *Italia*, the culinary culture shock was enough to last me a lifetime. I know for a fact that the food there is quite different from what we in the States recognize as "Italian" food. I know that my grandmother never changed the family recipes. She passed them down to us as they were given to her. So, who changed?

Do you know what they give you when you order pepperoni pizza in Italy? You will be amazed. Do you know what you have to go through to find a restaurant that serves minestrone soup? Stay tuned! Do you know where you will find the best pizza in Italy (hint-hint: It is where pizza was invented)?

Yes, there actually were some dishes that I liked very much, such as the Penne Pasta Arrabiata. And the Neapolitan pizza with no cheese! That's right, I said no *formaggio*.

. . .

"You have to be flexible," said Jera when I asked her about the strikes. I couldn't help but become increasingly dumbfounded by the almost predictable, unpredictable disruptions to one's daily routine caused by labor stoppages—bus strikes, train strikes, postal strikes. Half-day strikes. Two-hour strikes. I was told that strikes are common in Italy because the powerful labor unions and government workers are able to use these walkouts as leverage in contract talks. It is their main weapon against cutbacks. A short, spontaneous hit-and-run walkout is often more disruptive than a long, drawn-out strike.

"You have to be flexible." Certainly, it would do no good to be anything but. One day, after I had lived in Italy six weeks, I walked all the way from school to the apartment due to a bus strike, a distance of three to four miles.

> *Today is another typical day in Italy. Sciopero! (<u>SHAW</u>-PAY-ROA) That means strike. They do it all the time. Today there is a postal strike (but just for today). Also, the server is down (and has been since Friday), which may or may not have something to do with the postal strike. So I cannot get to my email and have not the slightest clue as to when I will be able to. Last week there was a general train strike for 24 hours. The week before there was a four-hour bus strike that was changed to a two-hour strike by the time it happened!*

As I sit here writing, months after having returned home from all those strikes, I discover a news item on the Internet about a parish church in Sicily that, yes... went on strike. The church suspended all ecclesiastical activities, except for the Last Sacrament!

4

CHEERS

On my way. My first trip outside the North American continent. How come Grandpa never went back, I wondered? Hmmmm... oh, well. *Salute!* Or, as some would say, *cin cin* (CHIN CHIN)!

Gloria and I drove from Dayton to the Greater Cincinnati airport (actually in Kentucky) where we joined my dad and stepmother who came to see me off. There we had a beer and a bite to eat at a place called Cheers, a theme bar patterned after the TV show of the same name. No, we didn't see Sam or Rebecca or Woody there, but the decor was genuinely reminiscent of the Boston pub so popular for many seasons in American homes, a fitting spot for a celebration. Every so often the wait staff would come together, go to the foyer outside the entrance. and do a lively dance. People walking through the concourse would stop to watch. It was fun! It made me wonder what kind of celebration and fun awaited on the other side of the Atlantic.

Classes would not begin until the third week of September, so I did not *have* to leave as early as I did on that last day of August. Still, I thought it was probably important to take the same flight from New York's Kennedy Airport as the American students were taking. This would help me become better acquainted with the students in the program and enable me to participate in the intensive language and culture classes being offered those first few weeks. By arriving together, we could become acclimated and culture shocked together!

One aspect of culture shock I was eager to avoid was that of having my pockets picked clean by the notorious gypsies who undoubtedly were lying in wait to fleece some stupid, unsuspecting *Americano* like me. Having been amply warned about this potentiality, I had left my billfold at home and opted instead to carry on my person two black leather pouches to hold my passport, credit cards, ATM card, money, and travelers' checks. These clever zippered pouches (also known as *Hidden Wallets* or *Securitypaks*) attach conveniently to one's belt and can be tucked inside the pants, out of sight. With these I felt secure, barring the chance that someone would manage to run off with my pants—belt, pouches and all!

The only baggage I checked through was a backpack and a large suitcase. Crammed solid, they felt like they weighed a hundred pounds. Gloria—bless her heart—had helped me pack, carefully folding, rolling, and wrapping stuff to minimize wrinkling and squeezing stuff into every little space to make for a snug fit.

There were so many things to remember that I even made up a checklist (see appendix) of the most important items so I wouldn't forget them. Most of these, including the camera and borrowed laptop, I carried with me on the plane, either inside a leather briefcase or on my person.

It was on the flight from Cincinnati to New York that I discovered the journal with a card for good wishes that Gloria had secretly slipped inside my briefcase. She surprised me, as she has on so many occasions! It was an attractive hardcover diary with a depiction of the Leaning Tower on the cover along with the words: *Italy: A Journal--The Reflective Traveler.* Written inside: "To Mi Pietro--with all my love. Buon Viaggio! Gloria."

I actually used the journal only sporadically. Still, the thought and the sentiment were appreciated. While on the plane, I penned my first entry:

> *What a nice surprise--this journal! As we take off from Cincinnati, about an hour late, I discover the journal and a card. How neat! I got teary-eyed. There's an empty seat next to me, Gloria, why aren't you in it? Ha! Ha!*

The reason for the delay, we were told while sitting on the runway, was that there were security problems in New York, thus, incoming flights were backed up.

. . .

At Kennedy, I saw a familiar face. It was Jill, the one student in the program from my own school. We had been introduced early in the year, then met several times to compare plans for the trip, sharing information and talking about what we thought it might be like "over there."

When I spotted her, we happened to be in line at a counter near the gate. She introduced me to Jen, a student from the other university in Dayton. The waiting line was in a state of disarray—more like a crowd than a line, a line that included a number of Italians and folks of other nationalities.

I overheard a comment by a person with a British accent who remarked that Italians "obviously don't know how to stand in line." It was true. There was no line. Everybody was helter-skelter, pushing and shoving, darting in front of one another, children, baby buggies, and baggage included. What was I getting myself into?!

When I finally got to the gate, a dumpy part of the terminal, there wasn't much else to see or do. The only food service nearby was an unkempt Burger King, hardly fitting fare for such a special occasion.

. . .

According to Rand-McNally, it is 4,278 miles from New York to Rome. That's a mile for every type of pasta you will find once you get there. The metric equivalent is 6,883 kilometers, which is important to know because once you arrive in Italy you quickly discover that no one understands anything about miles, or pounds, or inches. It's like the people there live in a different world! Most don't even understand English! I am being facetious, of course, but you don't know how 'foreign' a foreign country can be until you go there.

My plane was headed not to Rome, however, where so many international flights touch down, but to Malpensa, an airport near Milan in the north of Italy, an hour and a half driving time from my ultimate destination, the Savoyian city of Torino.

I would venture to say that most Americans do not know where Malpensa or Milan or Torino is located. I mean Rome, Florence, Venice, and even Sicily are familiar to many in the U.S.A. for various reasons. Conversely, few Italians I met recognized or knew anything about Ohio. But they all knew and seemed to have a special place in their hearts for New York and California.

In all fairness to the Italians, we Americans do a pretty poor job learning the geography of our own country—those in the East envisioning those nameless big square states out West, unable to distinguish one from the other. Folks living east or west of the Mississippi, respectively, not knowing much about locations or distances of states on the other side of the country.

Ohio or Iowa? How could one possibly confuse the two? Back in the 1980's I did a visiting professorship at Cal Poly in San Luis Obispo, California. I was there for three months. When the term was over, two male students came by the faculty office to wish me well on my trip back home. "Have a good trip back to Iowa," said one, after which he was quickly nudged and corrected by the other—"Not Iowa, dummy! Ohio."

. . .

Delta flight 84 departed Kennedy at 6:25 P.M. and would arrive at Malpensa at 8:30 the next morning. Allowing for the six-hour time difference, the actual flight would take eight hours. The plane was a Boeing 767 wide-body jet with a capacity of 218 passengers, and only a few empty seats. Mine was an aisle seat in economy class along the far right side of the plane where the seats run two abreast next to the window. It was about as comfortable as one could ask to be, considering the length of the flight.

I don't like long flights. I got no more than an hour's worth of sleep on the plane, while instead watching part of a movie, studying my Italian, drinking a Bloody Mary, eating a lot, and talking with some of the students and other people. As I attempted to converse with a young Italian by the name of Philippe, my first chance to try out his native language was inconclusive due to the deafening roar of the engines.

I was seated next to Charles, one of the American students on the study abroad program. As it would turn out, Charles was going to be living with an Italian family about two blocks from the apartment where I would be staying. Consequently, he and I would often ride the same bus to and from school, and sometimes meet in the evening at the Big Ben Pub in the neighborhood of the Piazza Guala to study our Italian lesson.

Charles was an interesting and unusual young man. A few years older than the other students, he was avidly into hiking, mountain climbing, and soccer. Within a few weeks of our arrival he would become a fan of Juventus, the elite Torino soccer team.

Charles had already completed a four-year college degree so why, I asked, was he pursuing the study abroad program? He said he was "trying to find himself." He really wanted to obtain a job in Italy, perhaps in a museum where he could immerse himself in Italian art. During the weeks and months to come I would learn a lot from Charles—from his experience with the Italian family of four he stayed with, from the little discoveries he would make in exploring the landscape of Torino, and from his keen perceptions of the people and the language. For example, he would relate how the boy in the Italian family was so spoiled that it was upsetting for him to observe. The mama would do everything for the son, but not for the daughter. One day the son is just lying on the sofa watching TV and yells for someone to come shut the window in the living room. Mama has to interrupt her cooking to go into the next room and shut the window for this lazy, pampered son.

This would not be the first time I would learn something from a student. One of the hidden perks of being a professor is the realization that learning is a two-way street. Like during the weeks and months preceding my departure, when I got much unsolicited advice from students I didn't even know. Some would hear of my upcoming trip and stop by the office to share their experiences, or to tell me about someone they knew who knew someone who had been to Italy, giving me tips on where to go and what to see. Jorge, for example, had apparently thoroughly enjoyed his trip to *Italia*. He brought me books and maps and offered to be a resource in anyway he could. He said he made a practice of buying tour books wherever he was visiting abroad instead of having to be encumbered by a camera. I could identify with that.

After Charles and I finished talking, I tried to catch a few winks, but it was a losing battle. The plane moved further out over the Atlantic, with depictions of our location relative to the ocean and landmasses flashing on the big screen. Maybe I was afraid I would miss something. If I had any feelings of anxiety about the flight or what lay ahead, I tried not to entertain them but instead chose to focus my thoughts on the gala events of the past year. I reflected especially on the best friends and family a man could ever have, the people who helped me get this far.

There was Rory, Head of International Programs at Wright State who gave me lots of guidance on how to write a winning proposal. And it worked, as I became the first faculty from my school to be awarded a Consortium appointment.

There was Bruno, the Italian instructor and native of Venice. From him I learned more than enough Italian to get by, plus a lot about the history, culture, and customs.

There were Terry and Caroline whom we met in the Italian class and, by strange coincidence, who actually had contacts in Torino where I was headed. They even helped me find a reasonably priced apartment there, and introduced me to the gracious and amicable contact person, Giuseppina.

To all these kind and kindred souls, I am deeply indebted. But most of all, to my family. It may sound trite to say that I am blessed to have such a warm and wonderful family, but it is true! When I would tell people in Italy that I had five children, they apparently thought I was crazy! Their silence and lack of any sign of expressive approval said it all. But don't Italians have large families? Not these days, I learned, and especially not in the north. In fact, Italy has already achieved zero population growth, and is actually facing a shrinking population.

Why this is so, I am not sure, but as one observer of the Italian scene suggests—facetiously, perhaps—the complexity of the Italian bureaucracy may be a causal factor. In a published guide for Americans and other foreigners wanting to get married in Rome, the array of procedures, documents, fees, verifications, and approvals necessary is mind-boggling.

Times change, of course. Even in the USA, it is much less fashionable today to have a large family than it once was. Back in 1960, when I first got married at the age of 20, large families were not unheard of, especially among Catholics. Aileen and I did not plan to have children for awhile, but we didn't plan not to, either. So, like good Catholics, we practiced the rhythm method. The results were astounding! Within 33 months, we were given our first three babies. By the time we figured out that the rhythm method didn't work, our family was complete with five beautiful, healthy children—Nancy (1961), Geno (1962), Steve (1963), Tom (1965), and Tony (1967)—who have never failed to make us anything but proud.

Now as any mother knows, when you have this many children so closely spaced, life is not a bowl of pasta fazoli! Yes, there were three in diapers at the same time. There were happy times and there were tough times but we always seemed to find a way. My dad was a steady and reliable presence when the kids were small. He was always eager to pitch in and help out, which he often did whether we asked for help or not. His love helped shape our values and our family traditions.

Today, more than thirty years after Tony was born, the kids are and will always continue to be an integral part of my life. Thus, it was no great surprise when all of them showed up, along with some friends and extended family, about a week before my departure for a *Buon Viaggio* Party. Saying goodbye is never easy but having a party to soften the blow doesn't hurt.

For about a month preceding the trip, we enjoyed farewell dinners with family and friends, lifting our glasses, and drinking toasts, "*Salute*!" It was almost like an extension of the celebration of a year earlier at the time of my marriage to Gloria. And the celebration would continue, even after the return from Italy. Geno would pick us up at the airport, and upon arrival at our house, we would promptly discover that

Steve had already been there and gone, having decorated several rooms with streamers, balloons, and banners shouting "Welcome Home."

. . .

If ever there was a cause for celebration—a wedding, a Christening, a birthday, a trip to Italy...this was it. As the plane approached the European Continent, I felt like I was following in my grandpa's footsteps, in reverse, of course. He was the real pioneer. Often in my lifetime I have felt a close sense of identification with him, with his pioneering and adventurous spirit. Relocating the whole family to a new country on a distant continent, back in the days before air travel—now *that* was pioneering.

Much of the history has been lost. What I know: Grandpa sailed from Italy to the USA (and back again) somewhere between five and 12 times. He would come here to work and make some money, and prepare a place to eventually settle the family. And, in the process, he also learned how to become an American citizen with the help of a cousin who preceded him and acted as a support. This was all prior to 1928, the year Grandpa brought the whole family over, including my dad, on a ship called the *Conte Bianco*. So, he did go back many times, and we believe that he was actually commuting!

Those were the days of Mussolini, and I am told that the first family member Grandpa brought to the States was the eldest son, my Uncle Ralph, because they wanted to draft him into *Il Duce's* army. It was between 1925 and 1929 that the Italian state was transformed into a dictatorship under Mussolini, with the slogan "Everything within the state. Nothing outside the state. Nothing against the state." Grandpa thought otherwise. He was no dummy! He saw the handwriting on the wall and wasn't about to hang around for what was going to happen to Italy under the Fascists. Eventually, he brought the whole family here and they automatically became citizens because he had become one first. Then he never went back again.

I believe Grandpa was typical of the Italians who migrated to the USA in the early part of the 20th century. Most came from the south, as opposed to the north, and most came from small towns rather than large cities. The Carusone hometown is called Bellona, not to be confused with the northern city of Bologna, and is about 20 miles north of Naples.

I think Grandpa would have preferred to settle in a small town here in the States, like Seneca Falls, New York, where some of the cousins reside to this day. But, as fortune would have it, when he arrived the job opportunities were in Cincinnati.

What would Grandpa have to say about my trip were he still alive? I felt certain that wherever he was he would be with me during my journey. He would know my thoughts, hopes, and fears. He would help guide me, or at least watch in amusement as I fumbled my way through this strange country, the land where he was born and raised.

It is difficult to say precisely what I hoped to find when the plane touched down. After all I had read and learned about Italy, from what I thought I knew about what it meant to be Italian...still, there was a sense of uneasy anticipation. Was this a dangerous place? Would I be readily accepted? Would anyone care that a Carusone had returned?

I know I had a certain mind set about the traditions and customs I would be looking for. Visions of Italian camaraderie, music, fun, and dancing. Loud, animated conversation. A chance to meet Italian families, maybe connect with some Carusones.

What I did not know was that I was in for some real surprises. There would be times when I would wonder "Is this really Italy?" and "Whatever happened to...?" and "Don't they know how to make...?" I did not know that instead of shouting Cheers or *Salute* when drinking a toast, the Italians would say, "*Cin Cin*" (CHIN CHIN).

5

THAT'S ITALIAN!

I was named after my grandpa. But so were four of my cousins! Now how many Pete Carusones are enough?

It is an Italian tradition. The first-born son is named after the paternal grandfather. Since my dad's parents had five sons and two daughters who survived beyond childhood, and since every son got married and had at least one son, and since my grandfather's name was Pietro, how many Pete Carusones does that make? Five. Right! So far, so good! Now, keeping in mind that I have four sons and a daughter, and all four of my sons have at least one son, how many more Pete Carusones does that make? Wrong! None of my sons named a son after me. They broke the family tradition!

There is only one thing worse and that is the fact that there actually is a sixth Pete Carusone who is the son of one of my cousins Pete. You see, this cousin named his son after himself instead of after his father. He didn't get it! We always thought he was a little *pazzo* (crazy) anyway. He probably didn't understand, or didn't like his dad's name (which is Americo), as he named his boy after himself and, of course, no self-respecting Italian would do that!

In retrospect, I kind of understand my sons' decisions to name their sons other names. Kind of. I mean, how many Pete Carusones are enough? Sure, it creates confusion at family gatherings. It saddens me, though, not so much because there are no grandsons named after me, but more so because it discontinued a meaningful and proud legacy that I think will become more important to my sons as they grow older. And because I have such fond memories of my grandpa. Who knows, maybe someday the grandsons will revive the tradition.

I used to joke with the kids about this matter. Since my youngest son, Tony, would be the last to marry and have children, I would say that I decided to leave my whole estate (if you can call it that) to the son who names his first born son after me. Which, of course, meant that Geno, Steve, and Tom had already lost out! However, Tony didn't take the bait—he and Carrie named their first son Anthony.

. . .

In my early years I was not raised in an atmosphere of *bona fide* Italian culture, despite the fact that both my parents were full-blooded Italian. Mother and Dad were quite Americanized. They never spoke Italian around the house and Mother cooked mainly American dishes—so that to a great extent my early exposure to Italian culture came from grandparents, aunts, and uncles. One exception to this was the way mother and dad dressed me for school, keeping in mind that the formality of 'dressing up' is very much an Italian thing. (Even today, American tourists are conspicuous by their baggy jeans, tennis shoes and *University* sweatshirts.)

The grade school I attended, Saint Francis Seraph, is in an uptown neighborhood of Cincinnati called Over the Rhine, which had a rich history of early German immigration. I walked the five blocks to school everyday, usually with a boy named Robert who lived nearby.

Mother and dad must have done a pretty good job of seeing to it that I was well dressed because of an incident I recall when Sister (all the teachers were nuns in those days) without warning decided to use me as a role model on how to dress. She called me up in front of the class which, of course, scared the heck out of me because I had no idea what I had done! Then she proceeded to tell the other boys, most of whom were wearing blue jeans, how much nicer it looked to wear dress slacks, using me as an example! Well, you can imagine my embarrassment and--not only that but--anxiety, too, that I might not make it home that day in one piece.

When I was 10, my parents divorced. Dad and I moved from our uptown Cincinnati neighborhood and in with Grandpa Pietro, Grandma Matilde and two of my dad's unmarried brothers who were still living at home, a typical Italian custom. This was a very different but also positive environment compared to what I had experienced before. Instead of having a baby sister seven years my junior in the house (in retrospect, of course, it's regrettable that I never got the chance to grow up with my sister and get to know her, even though my dad and I would take her out and do stuff together on weekends), now I would have two older uncles, namely, Uncle Ralph and Uncle Americo.

And other aunts and uncles and cousins were always dropping in, so it was a bustling household with a kind of party-like atmosphere. I usually had someone to play with or talk to if I wanted or, if I didn't want to, I could spend time up in the attic or out in the yard by myself. Or with the family dog—didn't every Italian family have a dog?

Uncle Ralph was the eldest and Uncle Americo the youngest, with about 20 years separating them. A quiet and thoughtful man, Uncle Ralph was "on the serious side," but when he had something to say, others would listen, perhaps because he was the oldest. Uncle Ralph's mustache didn't quite meet the corners of his lips, and you could start to see his scalp showing thru his receding hairline. Every morning I watched him stir a raw egg into a cup of black coffee, then down it all in one big gulp. He played the mandolin and loved to sing. He was a good billiard player, and served in the U.S. Army in the early 1940s. Uncle Ralph and my grandpa often hunted together, which accounted for the several stuffed pheasants decorating the living room.

Uncle Americo, also known as "Mingo," aka "Tony," aka "Emric," and sometimes simply "M," was only 10 years my senior and more like a big brother than an uncle. He played the piano (his favorite was the "boogie woogie"), and was a good jitterbug (swing) dancer. He's always had a great sense of humor and is a fun person to be around. His real name, Americo, came from his being the only one of the siblings to be born in America, right after the family's arrival. In fact, Grandma was pregnant with him when they came over on the boat.

Whenever letters arrived from Italy, there would be much excitement and animated discussion. Uncle Pat, the banker, would be called upon to do the translation. Whenever something important happened on the national or international news front, there would be much excitement and animated discussion. In fact, whenever something happened to almost anybody—or so it seemed—there would be much excitement and animated discussion. That's one of the things I was looking for in Italy, that emotional vitality and explosiveness.

There were traditions and rituals in the *Carusone familia* that you could count on as surely as Monday follows Sunday. One of these, fairly common among lots of Italian-American families, was menu planning. Every Thursday and every Sunday were pasta nights. That meant spaghetti or mostaccioli (penne) or some other variety of pasta, plus meatballs or *bragiola* (a kind of rolled, stuffed round steak, baked and served in a red sauce), a garden salad, maybe a vegetable or potato, lots of fresh baked Vienna bread from the neighborhood German bakery, and fruit, cakes, and cookies. Tuesday was often, but not always, a pasta night. Then on Fridays and Mondays, the usual fare would be either pasta fagioli (pasta with beans) or something like broccoli and beans, or cooked cabbage, or fish. The menu on Wednesdays and Saturdays I don't recall, but it had to be fast because Uncle Americo had his own rituals—bowling on Wednesday night, going to the movies with his buddies on Friday night, and a date, when he could find one, on Saturday.

Grandma often chided him in her soft-spoken, broken English to spend more time at home. (That's the way Italian and Jewish mothers are, right?) But Uncle M was always easygoing and with his great sense of humor made it hard for her to get really upset with him. She would act like she was, but he could turn on the charm and get her to laugh quite easily. Of course, she knew she was being conned, and I can still see the final scene: Grandma waving her hands and yelling something at him in Italian as Uncle M grabs his coat and slips out the door.

It took awhile for me to adjust to this new setting. As with most kids who go through the divorce process (parents usually think of it as *their* divorce, not the kids'), there were some really rough times, which I mainly kept to myself. Ironically, when I was young there were aspects of Italian culture, like some of the unfamiliar foods, the language, and the braggadocio, that I did not appreciate . I wanted to be "American." I didn't care about all that Italian stuff. Grandma and Grandpa usually spoke in their native tongue, even when talking with my dad and his brothers and sisters. However, most of the Italian words I can remember are better not repeated here!

. . .

Grandpa was the first Pietro. Or at least the first one known to me. He spent lots of time in his garden up on the hill. He had a grape arbor in the backyard above the concrete patio. He made wine. Everyone was his friend—the mailman, the milkman, the newspaper carrier. He would often invite them in for a cup of coffee or something stronger. And at Christmastime there would be that bottle of homemade red for them to take home.

Grandpa liked watching TV, his favorites being boxing, the Ed Sullivan show, and singers like Kate Smith and Mario Lanza. He enjoyed playing cards, at home with the family and out with friends. Even in his later years, about once a month, my Uncle Pat would drive him to a tavern in the Findlay Market area on a Saturday night where he would meet some of his old cronies in the backroom where they would play poker and pinch the women. I used to wonder just how much Grandma knew.

As a parent, Grandpa was a strict but loving disciplinarian. And he taught his kids to take care of themselves. Now, it is not unusual for immigrant families to have problems acclimating, especially when other kids in the neighborhood tease the young ones. Shortly after the family arrived from Italy, for example, someone taught my dad some cuss words in English and told him that it meant "Good Morning, Sister." The result—Dad was punished by having to kneel on the nun's keys (ouch!).

Since dad and his brothers were increasingly getting into fights with other kids, grandpa sent them to the Friars Club to learn boxing. My dad did so well that he would become a Golden Gloves Scholastic Champion.

A couple years after we moved in with my grandparents, Grandma had a stroke and it was decided to move to a larger house so the daughters could be there around the clock. Talk about a closely knit family! It was a yellow brick three-story house out in the suburbs with a nice yard and our very own driveway. Grandma and

Grandpa, Uncle Americo, Uncle Ralph, my dad and I occupied the apartment on the first floor. Aunt Millie, Uncle Dominic, and cousin Vince lived on the second floor while Aunt Rose and Uncle Pat lived on the third floor. There was always someone at home and something to do.

Almost every Sunday we would line up the cars (about five of them) in the driveway and everyone would pitch in, working together, washing and waxing each other's cars. By now I was going to Roger Bacon, an all boys' Franciscan high school, and working in Uncle Dominic's dry cleaning store after school and on Saturdays. I did that for five years, learned a lot from Uncle Dominic in the process, and helped pay my way through school.

When grandma died, the family split up and moved. Aunt Millie and Uncle Dom bought a house and took Grandpa with them. I went to live with my godparents, Aunt Rose and Uncle Pat, who never had any children of their own and who rented a nice apartment. Since my dad was going to be renting a small flat and living a single life, everybody thought I would be in a better environment with my aunt and uncle. They were right, of course, although I may not have fully realized it at the time. I still saw my dad quite a bit and talked with him on the phone every night. It was just another phase in my growing up.

. . .

Aunt Rose and Uncle Pat were very good to me, treating me like the child they never had. Everyone said Aunt Rose "has a big heart," as if to excuse some of her more obvious shortcomings, such as the fact that she was fanatic and compulsive, especially about things like housecleaning, laundry, and being neat and tidy. When we all lived together she would often do the laundry for Grandma, washing clothes for all of us—for my uncles, my dad, and me as well. That's how she earned the nickname "Clorox Rose" (thanks to Uncle Americo) because she would use so much bleach in the wash that our underwear was falling apart!

Aunt Rose was kind of superstitious and strongly opinionated about many things. With an abiding faith in the power of angels and saints, she kept a small shrine on a table in the corner of her bedroom complete with votive candles, statues, and pictures of Jesus, Mary, and the saints. She had a very loud, penetrating voice and in public places would often say embarrassing things. Everybody loved her but sometimes her manners would wear thin. She wore her emotions on her sleeve and had a flair for the dramatic, much like *Lucilla* of Tim Parks' *Italian Neighbors*.

Aunt Rose and Uncle Pat introduced me to the activities of the Italian-American community in Cincinnati. There were pasta dinners and dances with live music at the Italian Church downtown that were enjoyed by people of all ages; the annual Italian Day picnic at Coney Island amusement park on the Ohio river; and the formal Columbus Day dinner-dance every October, always well attended by judgeship and political candidates who wished to win the votes of the Italian-American community. These were family events and always occasions for celebration, many of which were sponsored by the United Italian Societies, or by one of its constituent fraternal orders such as the Roman Knights or the Order Sons of Italy in America.

. . .

Many other things stand out from my Italian-American upbringing, and I look back on these with fond memories:

- As a baby, being rubbed with olive oil (something I've been told, not that I remember).
- Family gatherings, with card playing (usually for nickels and dimes), loud talking and shouting, music and dancing.

- Easter dinner blessings with palm leaves and holy water, and specially baked bread in the form of a cross with eggs nestled in the four ends.
- Going to Mass and taking Holy Communion.
- Being called names, like dago and wop.
- The story about my dad sticking up for his sister and getting into a fight with the priest because she had decided to have her wedding in a different parish.
- Always celebrating...birthdays, weddings, and anniversaries, holidays, Christenings and graduations, *"salute!"*
- Iced coffee, torrone candies, Stella Doro cookies, spumoni ice cream, home made pasta noodles, pizza from scratch, anisette.
- "Mangia, mangia, eat!" Always. "What's wrong? You don't like it?"
- Helping grandpa make homemade wine, a family project that took place once a year in his basement and supplied enough for everyone for the next 12 months.
- Italian weddings with thousands of homemade Italian cookies, and confetti candies (Jordan almonds in white or pastel colors: the fresh almonds have a bittersweet taste, representing life, while the white sugarcoating is added so that the newlyweds' life will be more sweet than bitter). Also, a live band at the reception with everyone doing the bunny hop and dancing the *Tarantella* and *Return to Sorrento*.

Of course, not everyone who grew up as an Italian-American has had the same experiences I did, I'm sure. Everybody's background is bound to be somewhat different. But, chances are that 80 to 90 percent of the things discussed in this chapter would be familiar to others of Italian-American descent. They are things, I would venture to say, that even non-Italians in the USA would often relate to as being "Italian."

And when you are raised in such an environment of warmth and hospitality and love, with an overriding sense of family and camaraderie, and a gusto for the joy and celebration of life, what more would you expect from people in the real Italy? Nothing more, and nothing less.

6

ARRIVAL

Torino (or Turin), the Detroit of Italy. First capital of Italy. Home of the Holy Shroud and the world champion soccer team, Juventus FC, a brand of Fiat.

Flying over the Alps as you approach Italy is an incredible and indelible experience. The stark beauty of those immense snow-capped mountains and majestic peaks surpasses anything I have ever seen. Those flying into Malpensa would have the opportunity to enjoy this surrealistic view, if they were seated by a window, that is, on their way to Torino, Milan, Como, or other places due north.

The plane stopped on an apron near the runway, some distance from the terminal building. Modern shuttles, low to the ground bus like vehicles built for standing only, came and took us the rest of the way. There was no welcoming committee, no marching band to greet us, not that I expected one. Only the *dogana* (Italian customs) and baggage claim. Then, to wait for our contact person, Mark, to arrive from the school.

A customs officer intercepted and questioned my friend, Charles. We think it was because his hair was long and straggly and, like many Italian males, his face was unshaven, so maybe they thought he wasn't an American like the rest of us. I had to show my passport but no one asked for a visa or how long I was planning to stay. That was a relief.

The airport was clean, quiet, and rather cozy. We camped outside a coffee bar in a corner near the offices of the Carabinieri. Uniformed guards would come and go, carrying their automatic guns, looking authoritarian and very serious. At one point our piles of luggage were partially blocking the doorway to their office, something they did not seem too pleased about. I was concerned about the luggage being secure, as some of the students had taken off to who knows where while others were having coffee nearby, and it would be more than a couple of hours before we were to depart for Torino. Already I felt like a mother hen and hadn't even met all the students yet!

Finally, in came the bus from Torino and on it was Mark. The first thing he did was to make sure everyone was accounted for (actually one student had missed his flight from Frankfurt and wound up getting lost), and then to see if there were enough tickets for everyone for the return trip. Now you have to understand that the buses between Torino and Malpensa run only two or three times a day. The trip takes about an hour-and-a-half, and then the bus lays over for a couple of hours. So it was important to make sure there was space for everyone on this bus. Otherwise, some would have to hang around the airport for another six hours, waiting.

The countryside on the bus ride to Torino, my first real glimpse of Italy, was interesting but not spectacular. As we passed farmhouses and villages, I could see mountains in the distance, and as we approached the city, industrial and commercial buildings and many tall apartment buildings began to appear.

In downtown Torino we were greeted by Jera, the director of the studies abroad program who told us to be prepared to meet again in the morning for a tour of the city. Then she promptly dispatched us by a fleet of private cars and taxis to our respective housing destinations. We were all pretty exhausted and eager to go someplace to relax and get settled.

My first impression of Torino confirmed what I had learned about the city before leaving the States, namely, that it is a large bustling, congested place with people piled on top of each other and traffic racing everywhere. Unlike other large Italian cities, Torino has no subway system (*metropolitana*), thanks to the political clout of Fiat, the largest private employer in Italy and also the owner of the city's newspaper, *La Stampa*.

There was other information about Torino I had been exposed to prior to the trip, mostly from abstracts of news items on the Internet. These painted a picture of architectural beauty, but also of crime, corruption, and black magic:

A Turin for the better:
Italy's northern metropolis

Turin, Italy, is not a well-visited tourist destination, but those who discover the city enjoy its gentle beauty and muted personality.

Turin's Baroque Splendors

The Baroque architecture of Turin Italy is featured with emphasis on the Church of Santa Cristina on the Piazza San Carlo.

Shroud 1,800 years old?

Dmitri Kouznetsov, a Russian biochemist working for the Turin Shroud Center of Colorado in Colorado Springs, believes the Shroud of Turin dates back at least 1,800 years--making it much older than scientists have said.

Turin judges turn to sex and soccer

Turin, Italy, magistrates have opened a file on a corruption and bribery through sex scandal at Torino FC in their investigation of a "black fund" to pay for behind-the-scenes perks to players and provide prostitutes for referees and linesmen who officiate at Torino matches.

In fear and loathing.

In an article from Italy's "La Stampa," Ezio Mascarino examines the crime which is plaguing the city of Turin. Drug addiction, theft, and poverty are rampant in Turin, and many of the citizens feel they have no protection.

Do Devil and His Disciples Lurk in Turin?

Turin, Italy, has cultivated a reputation as a haven of the occult. The city is said to be the source of a special energy which attracts religion, white magic, black magic, and Satanism.

Italy Debates a Capital Idea--Down with Rome!

George Armstrong comments on Italy's debate to change its capital, using the arguments of Luigi Firpo, a history professor at Turin University, and Alberto Moravia, the dean of Italian novelists and native of Rome.

In the coming months I would experience the Torinese sense of political superiority owing to their special place in Italian history. I would encounter their disdain for people from the South but also the beautiful baroque architecture of their churches, palaces and public buildings, a fanaticism for soccer, and a deep sense of pride in the Holy Shroud. As for rampant crime and devil worship, these remained well hidden from my view.

. . .

The *Duomo* (cathedral) of San Giovanni where the Shroud is kept is named after Saint John the Baptist, patron saint of Torino. This famous edifice was built in the 15th century. It contains a fantastic exhibit detailing the features and history of the Shroud, highlighted by a backlit replica and some short videos. But the actual garment itself was not on display when I was there since that part of the church, like many other monuments and churches throughout Italy, was undergoing renovation.

In the days of the Roman Empire, Torino was a fortified outpost due to its strategic location on the River Po at the foothills of the mountains leading into France and Switzerland. An elegant Baroque city, Torino became the seat of the Savoy dynasty in the 16th century.

Today, it is the capital of the region of Piedmont, home of the second largest Egyptian Museum in the world, and offers a wealth of history, culture, and art. This is the land of truffle-hunting dogs, where vermouth was invented and some of the great wines of Italy like *Barbera* and *Asti* are still produced.

After two wars for independence, the first of which started in 1848, Torino became the first capital of Italy in 1861. That is when modern Italy officially became a nation, nearly a hundred years after the founding of the United States (of America). The first elections and parliament of the united Italy were held in that year also and Vittorio

Emanuele II was crowned King. In 1865 Italy's capital moved from Torino to Florence, and then five years later to Rome. Of course, some are of the opinion that even today "the boot" is still not a unified nation. Today, more than 130 years after Rome became the capital, some Italians in Milan and Torino are promoting a movement to relocate the capital back to the north.

. . .

    The taxi ride from downtown to my apartment in the south part of the city was *rapido*, not unlike cab rides I'd experienced in large cities back in the States, except that when we got to the suburbs, there *were* no suburbs!

    That was my first big surprise. To discover that in Torino, as well as in other towns and cities across Italy, the great majority of Italians actually live in apartment buildings as opposed to single family houses. They buy the apartments much like Americans buy condos, but otherwise they are just like apartment buildings. If you can imagine an American city, like Dayton or Cincinnati or Chicago, with almost solid 10-story residential buildings from the city center all the way out to the edge of the city, with no single-family houses or ranches or duplexes, you have imagined what Torino looks like.

    Population density in Italy is seven times that of the USA, and more highly concentrated within the cities. If you look at Italian housing development of the 1950's, you would see that land distant from the inner city was not developed because housing plans were not integrated with public transportation. This forced up demand for houses as near to the center of towns as possible, further contributing to overcrowding. Unlike the UK and USA, urban centers in Italy are still desirable places to live, shop and hang out.

    I was told that a "nice apartment" would go for $150,000 to $250,000 and up. They are not affordable for the average Italian. Often it takes three generations of a family (grandparents, parents, and some of the children) pulling together to be able to afford an apartment. And since they are in very short supply, families tend to hold onto them over the years, even when they may no longer be living there.

As the taxi neared *Piazza Guala* I knew that my *appartamento* must be nearby. Sure enough, there it was on a small rather obscure street by the name of Via Cercenasco, just two blocks from the piazza. Apparently, the taxi driver knew where he was going after all. He and I had exchanged small talk, mostly in Italian, and that helped boost my confidence about my ability to get by with what little I had learned. Jera had warned me in advance about how much the ride would cost, and how much to tip, so that I wouldn't be overcharged.

I felt like I already knew Giuseppina, the woman from whom I was renting the apartment, due to numerous e-mail messages we had exchanged during the previous months. She was a white-collar working woman with a decent command of the English language, but not always with the correct spellings. (In all of these emails throughout the book, I have chosen to use the original versions, rather than to impose corrections upon them, in the interests of preserving authenticity and allowing the reader to draw from the experience of communicating in a language other than one's own. No disrespect to the writer is intended.) Thus, our e-mails were been a mishmash of both Italian and English, discussing matters pertaining to the apartment but also tidbits here and there about the weather and other aspects of life in *Italia*.

Caro Professor Carusone, she had written the first time...

I am not so good in speaking your language too but I can speak italian very well! and I hope I can

> *answer your questions properly! I talked to my friend, the owner of the one-room apartment in Torino. She said it will be OK for the time you will be here. The apartment is small but comfortable and sunny. It is quite not to far from via Ventimiglia where you can go by bus. Is at the 2nd and last floor of a new house in a reasonable quite street in the South of the city. There is a bath room with shower, towels, and washing machine. All the forniture for cooking are inside, also stove and refrigerator, table and chairs. A low wall divide the cooking zone from the bedroom, where you can find a single bed with sheets, little desk and wardrobe. There is the telephone.*
>
> *Terry and Caroline told me that possibly your wife can join you for some time. A double bed can be arranged, but the room will become very little. The rent is 600.000 Italian Lire per months all included, plus telephone. I hope can evaluate something more about the apartment now. If you need any other information, please let me now.*

There was still one thing that bothered me. From what I had heard about the bathrooms and toilets in Italy, and upon scrutinizing every word in her description, I still had visions of a common, semi-public toilet down the hall! Or, maybe outside? So, I wrote back and asked, rather naively:

> *I know this may sound like a strange question but I would like to know in the bath room is there also a toilette and a sink?*

This was the answer I received:

Dear Peter,

Yes, there are! (Toilette and Sink) of course.

Giuseppina

. . .

Via Cercenasco, like a scene out of *42nd Street*, is in an aging urban neighborhood just oozing with character. The building where I was going to be staying, only three stories high unlike the others nearby, looked scruffy and untidy. There was graffiti spray-painted on the wall outside next to the stoop. And an electronic security lock on the front door so that, in order to enter the hallway, you have to press a buzzer for someone inside to release the lock and let you in.

My *appartamento* was on the second level (*secondo piano*) which means two flights up, or what we would call the third floor. The second floor is called the first level because it is one flight up (*prima piano*), while the first floor is called the ground floor (*terra*). See?!

The owner was anxiously awaiting my arrival. I lugged my heavy bags up the stairway. The condition of the hallway was as unkempt and in need of paint as the exterior of the building. In contrast, it was a big relief to see how nice the apartment itself was. Quite small but, "so cute," as Gloria would say when she arrived weeks later.

Bright and cheerful, with three large windows, and a skylight in the kitchen, the decor was light and colorful. Appliances were quite small but functional and more than adequate for one person. It was almost ideal! Let's see, on the downside, there was a cooking range but no oven or microwave, and only a small TV that barely brought in a blurry picture on two or three channels.

Giuseppina had yet to arrive so I was on my own with the owner who spoke virtually no English. She was a delightful, spry, thin, grandmotherly type who proceeded to give me a personal tour and detailed explanation, in Italian of course, of every single thing in the place. She had a warm and engaging smile and I could tell from the glimmer in her eyes that she was genuinely glad to have this opportunity to welcome me. She explained and demonstrated the door locks, the stove, the washing machine, the shower, the refrigerator, the TV, the hot water heater, and everything else in the one room efficiency, smiling amicably as we inched along. Much of what she said went over my head as she was talking at lightning speed but I would nod my head anyway, as if I understood, and try to ask a question now and then so as to appear tuned in. She was so nice! She even showed me some soda pop she'd put in the refrigerator for me.

When Giuseppina finally arrived, I was able to straighten out the few things I still didn't understand, then make arrangements to pay the rent as soon as I could find a bank and get some cash. Giueseppina, nicely dressed in a business suit and probably in her 30s, was cordial but more formal. She offered to be of help, as needed, although her English was not as fluent as I had thought it would be. I believe she was disappointed that my Italian was not better than it was. She gave me her home and work numbers in case there was any problem. Also, instructions for keeping track of the telephone bill, and how to operate the butane tank that fueled the cooking range.

. . .

Those first few days the students and I saw a lot of Torino. That's when Jera gave her annual "pep talk" to the new students, laying out strict rules alongside motherly advice to guide their behavior during the coming months. To the *ragazze* (girls), especially, the advice was pointed: "Don't even look at an Italian man or he will take that as a yes! Don't pay any attention to him (even to say no) or he will take that as a sign of encouragement." It was interesting. "Italian men think foreign women are easy," she warned.

Jera had chartered a bus for the tour and while she and the Italian bus driver (a male) were carrying on a loud, argumentative power struggle—all in rapid-fire Italian, of course—we were enjoying the view of the city as well as the banter. They were arguing about the best direction to take and where to park the bus, I think. Apparently, Italian men don't like taking orders from a woman.

When we finally got underway, we saw so much—Torino's beautifully landscaped parks, monuments, and historic landmarks, its unusual Baroque architecture, and a lively and dynamic downtown shopping district. We toured the Superga—a big church with a fascinating history situated high on a hill overlooking the city where a famous battle was once fought: a Piemontese military commander facing overwhelming odds against the French promised the Blessed Virgin that if she would let him win the battle then he would in her honor build a church at that exact spot overlooking the city. She did and, the battle won, he kept his promise. We also toured the Piazza San Carlo, probably the most beautiful of the open, public squares in Torino, right in the heart of the downtown, and enjoyed wonderful pastries and cappuccino at a sidewalk cafe there. And we visited Parco Valentino, a big public park along the river just south of the downtown. It is a popular place to stroll and to take wedding pictures—maybe Mark, who was an American grad student here at one time and who now has an Italian girl he wants to marry, will find himself here on his wedding day.

. . .

I was "learning fast," I wrote home: I was spending a lot of time with Mark and Charles and Jera, Mark now working with Jera on the staff. He and I got along fine--I would help him and he helped me. Jera had taken me to a mall and a supermarket shortly after I had settled in so that I could buy some stuff for the apartment. She took us all (including about 20 students) out for pizza one night, and of course, on a tour of the city. Since Charles was living with an Italian family about 2 blocks from where I lived, we often took the bus together in the mornings. Some evenings we visited a local bar for a couple of beers (berre) and studied our Italian together.

Beyond my study with Charles, I'd signed up for an Italian class that met every morning. I succeeded in getting my ATM card to work right at the school where there is a machine in the hall!! Mark and I rode the bus downtown one day and he showed me the main train station and how it works when you want to take a trip someplace.

"No, my box, has still not arrived," I wrote home. "Good ole UPS! hahahaha! The last we heard is that it's in Milan. Why they won't deliver it is beyond me!" I continued in my fax to elaborate on what I was seeing and feeling in my early exposure to Italian culture:

> *I think you would be surprised at how big and frenetic the city is here. I mean, this is not some little town where people lay back all day. Yes, they do know how to enjoy life but the people are piled on top of each other (60 million people in a country the size of one state). The cars constantly racing all over, no respect for pedestrians, they park anywhere like even on the sidewalk. I'm enjoying my exposure to all this but looking forward to seeing other parts of Italy, too.*

7

IL PROFESSORE

Most people don't have the foggiest notion of what a college professor does. Or the difference between "teacher" and "professor."

Ed, who had been on the marketing faculty with me at Xavier University, once related a conversation he'd had with the minister of his church. Ed and I had both taught a standard 12-hour load on the semester system. Ed was already very active in his church but his minister was trying to convince him to do even more. "Ed," he said, "you teach only 12 hours a week!" To which Ed cleverly responded, "Yes, Reverend, and you preach only one hour a week!"

Ever since I can remember, family and friends would have difficulty comprehending just what it is that a college professor does with all his spare time when he is only in the classroom for 12 hours or, in some schools, nine or even six hours each week. It is tough enough trying to explain *what* I teach—"Marketing, what's that?"—but to have to constantly justify the use of one's time! "You only have classes on Tuesdays and Thursdays? What do you do the rest of the week? It must be nice!"

Yes, it must be nice, or so I thought on that day many years ago when I first gave serious consideration to a career in academia. It must be nice...to spend one's work day leisurely interacting with others, discussing important issues of the day, teaching, reading, preparing lectures and grading papers mostly at one's own pace. And getting paid for it! "It must be nice to be a college professor," I thought.

Since then, of course, I have awakened to the fact that much of one's so-called "free time" is spent attending endless meetings, processing administrative paperwork, doing research and writing journal articles for publication, giving talks and doing other forms of professional and community service, preparing classes, designing and grading tests, reading student papers and, yes, also engaging in some internal politics about turf matters and inconsequential minutia—but only *rarely* discussing issues of real importance.

In Italy, I was *Il Professore Visitando* (the visiting professor). That was my standard "line." Whenever someone would expect an introduction, an identity, a reason for my being there, I would blurt out "*Sono professore visitando*." And, "*Sono Americano*," or "*dagli Stati Uniti*." Or sometimes simply, "*Sono straniero*" (I am a foreigner).

The program office to which I was assigned (USAC) was just one entity within the larger school known as SAA (School of Business and Administration). Thus, my work there revolved around a handful of American and Italian staff people, and the students in the program who were mostly Americans. With all due respect, the facilities were not quite of the caliber to which I had been accustomed in the States. And office space was sorely lacking. It would have been nice to have my own office, or at least a desk.

Someplace to store course materials and a place to grade papers. Ah, but that would have been asking... too much! Alas, I was *Il Professore Visitando*.

Unfortunately, there was little opportunity for interaction with the Italian faculty. They seemed pleasant enough but also came across as aloof and elitist. For example, upon entering the dining room of the school cafeteria you would right away see their special table in a special corner, complete with linen tablecloth, stemware, and a vase with flowers. They were usually attired in suit and tie and their behavior seemed cliquish. I, in contrast, ate at the regular tables with the students and dressed more casually, not wishing to insult the Italians but wanting not to be snobbish to my students, either. One of the American students would later refer to the Italian faculty as "the Gods."

In contrast, the staff people were more amicable and cordial. For example, the Italian secretaries I would pass in the halls would often nod and say *"Buon Giorno," "Buona Sera,"* or *"Salve."* "Salve" was a new one on me! I was familiar with "Buon Giorno" for morning and "Buona Sera" for afternoon and evening, for formal greetings. I was conversant with the use of *Ciao* for informal greetings that one would use with close friends or children. But, I had not heard the *Salve* before. It sounded like something right out of a Latin primer—I could just see Romans in the Forum greeting each other with hand raised, palm forward as a salute, *"Salve!"* In fact, isn't there a traditional Roman Catholic prayer or hymn called "Salve Regina," meaning Hail Queen?

Well, the use of Salve turns out to be an intermediate form of greeting, not very formal but not overly familiar. It makes sense when you think about it, once you understand the culture. Among the Italian professors, and indeed throughout Europe as a whole, "status consciousness" is an integral part of the culture and shows up as formality and protocol in both language and dress code. It is a matter of respect. It is customary, for example, to address a person by title. Take the case of the woman from whom I was renting the apartment. I had been told that she liked to be addressed as *Dottoressa*, because she had a degree. And the person who pulled some strings to get me a speaking engagement at the local chamber of commerce. He was simply referred to as *l'avvocado* (the lawyer).

This was fine except that often my mind was not able to work fast enough to evoke the response appropriate to the person's station in life. By the time someone would utter a greeting and I would think of what to reply, it was too late. They'd already passed me by.

. . .

The box I'd been waiting for finally arrived. My infamous box. A corrugated carton about 18" by 12" by 10" which took UPS three months to deliver from Ohio to Torino. And there it set, on the floor next to the table in Jera's office. In it, all my teaching stuff, including textbooks, tests, handouts, transparencies, videos, etc.

Jera's office was *the* center for the whole USAC program. About 15 X 18 feet, it contained virtually everything relevant to the program: Jera's desk, two phones, fax machine, student and visiting professor mailboxes, supplies and handouts, a mini library, a computer, and—oh, yes, my box. This is where everybody worked, too: Jera, Mark, and Andrea. And it's where many other people would hang out, including the part-time and visiting faculty, former students, friends and acquaintances, Jera's dogs and, of course, all the students.

Sometimes there would be several students and staff people in the office at the same time, thereby making it impossible to move around and access the stuff in my box. I would have to ask people to move so I could get into my box to prepare for class. Now, if Jera's office sounds like a zoo, consider the fact that it was also home for her cute little Yorkie by the name of Aida—a Yorkie she'd trained to sing opera. The dog almost got onto Funniest Home Videos, but that's another story. (I know Jera felt embarrassed about the lack of office space for the *professore visitando* and would be very upset if I neglected to relate how the situation improved markedly the year after I left. In fact, she and Mark sent me pictures of the beautiful new offices so I would believe them!) I believe you, Jera, I believe. But, how come you waited until *after* I left?)

I was never given a key to Jera's office to be able to get to my box when she was not in. But that was not a problem since the lock on her door was broken (*rotto*) anyway and could easily be opened with a few artful jiggles. Until the day they fixed it! Then, in panic, I had to get help from the school receptionist, a kindly mild-mannered gentleman by the name of Bogetti who had all the keys to all the doors in the school.

As for computers and media equipment, let me just say that I appreciate the help and courtesies extended by Lorenzo and others on the staff. Lorenzo was the computer guru of the SAA and, bless his heart, worked hard to bring the school's computer facilities into the twentieth century. (That's just a joke, Lorenzo, non fare troppo serio!) Actually, the computers in the student lab at the time were only 5–6 years out of date, and some staff had much newer models. Since I left I understand they have been catching up fast.

I have vivid memories of the days I spent working in Lorenzo's computer *laboratorio*. If he was ever out, I could borrow a key from Bogetti. The system was so slow and unreliable when trying to access the Internet and my e-mail that I eventually began to log on to two computers at a time. If one would lock up, at least I'd have a chance with the other one while rebooting the first! One day Lorenzo came in while I was doing this and cleverly said in his distinct Italian accent, "Ah, I see you are multitasking!" That's how Mark and I referred to it from that day forward.

. . .

Some of my fondest memories are associated with Jonna and Charlie, the husband-wife team who ran the school cafeteria and bar. They are the nicest people! "Why do you call your husband Charlie," I once asked Jonna, "instead of Carlo which is the Italian for Charles?" She said it was because when they met there was another Carlo in the crowd they hung with, hence she called him Charlie to avoid confusion.

The cafeteria was a very busy place for lunch. The Italian students and faculty far outnumbered our USAC group, so sometimes it was difficult to find a table. On top of that, people who worked in offices near the school would sometimes drop by for lunch. Once a month, Jera would reserve a long table for all of us to celebrate birthdays for those in the program whose birthday happened to fall in that month.

The procedure in the cafeteria went something like this. Upon entering, you checked out the daily menu board, scouted a table, then went to the register where Jonna would take your order and money. Then, you grabbed a place setting to put on your table (real knives and forks, no plastic) and waited for your name to be called. Five to fifteen minutes later, when your order was ready, you picked up your order and condiments at the counter.

My friend Charles would get so upset because the Italian students would stand around the counter rather than wait at their table, thereby blocking the way for anyone else. The most annoying thing about Italians, Charles would say when he was asked, was "the Italian students standing in front of the lunch counter waiting for their food to be served like cows at the trough and making it impossible for you to get to your lunch which is the only one that's actually ready."

Jonna and Charlie always gave me good service, even for my morning cappuccino. Maybe it was because they liked me, or because I was *il professore visitando*. I don't know. I do know that I liked the two of them and hope to see them again someday. The same goes for Lorenzo and Bogetti.

One day Jera announced that it was Jonna and Charlie's 10th wedding anniversary, so we decided to all march down to the cafeteria and sing Happy Anniversary to them. Since it was the middle of the afternoon, the dining room was empty except for a few people having an afternoon espresso.

Andrea, Mark, Jera, and I marched in singing Happy Anniversary to the tune of Happy Birthday. Charlie and Jonna were delighted. They sat down with us, brought out a bottle of sparkling wine, some cookies and candies, and we all proceeded to celebrate! It was one of those special moments that made all of the other petty annoyances worthwhile.

. . .

Jera was very helpful to me during my stay, both with the class schedule and with technical issues in the classroom. For instance, she was able to get me a Tuesday-Wednesday teaching schedule, which allowed me to enjoy three days in Sorrento (south of Naples) one week, a tour of Pompeii, an overnight trip with students and staff to the Italian Riviera, and some relaxation by the ocean. And when I experienced a problem with the VCR I was using in my classes, she came to the rescue. I had been told that the Italian VCR uses a different format than we use in the USA. So, months earlier I had sent some videos to the USAC headquarters to have them converted to the Italian system. But, when I made a test run in the classroom, I discovered to my dismay that in the process of conversion the recording speed had been set on slow, and the Italian VCR would not play back at that speed! Before I had time to panic, Jera got approval to buy a new VCR, one exclusively for USAC's use, that could handle a range of speeds and formats. Thanks, Jera!

. . .

Students are often curious about how I decided to go into teaching, or 'professoring,' as the case may be, and whether I had any "real world" experience. That's especially important in a business school because experience gives you examples to talk about and enhances your credibility. Without it, you can get bogged down in theory that has little basis in reality.

The answer to their question is "Yes." It was the early 60's and I was in my early 20's, working at the *Cincinnati Enquirer* in the Advertising Promotion and Research Department. Of the 1,000 company employees, only two of us, my boss and myself, knew anything about marketing research. All the salespeople in the advertising division would come to us for advice, and for facts and figures pertaining to their respective accounts. Discovering that I could actually explain some of this complicated stuff to other people, see their eyes light up and their heads nod in understanding—that felt really good. Maybe it was an ego trip, but that's how I got the teaching bug! If I could make research data intelligible to others (statistics are usually scary to most people)—numbers about markets and products and shopping habits—if I was good at explaining this stuff, then maybe I would have something to offer a roomful of students eager to learn about this exciting world called "marketing."

There was something else that attracted me to academia, namely, the belief that being a college professor carried with it more respectability and prestige than other jobs, though not as much in the States as is the case in Europe. This is something that would be good for me and for my family, I reasoned, and for future generations of the Carusone family.

I saw a parallel here with the adventures and risk-taking moves of my grandpa. Didn't he do something out of the ordinary and take chances by coming to this country so that future generations of the family might have a better life? Wasn't this a worthwhile path to be following, in my grandpa's footsteps?

To broaden my experience, I eventually left the newspaper for a research position in the home office of Federated Department Stores. All this time I was continuing my education as a part-time MBA student, taking classes at nights and on Saturdays. Thus, I was able to complete the BFA and MBA degrees before enrolling full-time in a Ph.D. program. Two and a half years after joining Federated, I left the business world and made a full-time commitment to graduate school.

When we moved to Columbus where I enrolled at The Ohio State University, my wife and I had our first four children with us. Two years later when we left, we had completed our litter of five. So, when young people complain about having to work their way through school, or have difficulty balancing studies and work schedule, I just smile, recalling how at one time I had a full schedule of both work and school plus helping my wife to raise a large family of small children!

• • •

There is another benefit—besides the pleasure of explaining the exciting world of marketing— to working in an academic environment. It has to do with being around young people all the time. This helps keep one young and tuned in to new ideas. The students at the *scuola* were no exception; they were a great bunch and I enjoyed them immensely.

Toward the end of the semester, they put together a yearbook with humorous pictures and comments about their experiences in Italy. For example, Nicole, a Californian, was fascinated with the Italian bathroom and Italian shutters:

> *What is it with the shades on the <u>outside</u> of the windows which lead you to believe that its 3 a.m. all morning long? One can sleep all day--it's impossible to wake up!*
>
> *I cannot understand the bathtubs that consistently <u>lack</u> shower curtains. So--either you get water all over the place, or you sit down and take a bath!*
>
> *Don't get the hotels--they give you a bidet in the hotel room, but don't give you a toilet???*

The students usually stayed in hostels or rooming houses where common bathrooms are not unusual. And, yes, the bathtubs—even freestanding ones—were often set up with a shower hose attachment but with no enclosure or curtain to contain the water!

Ken of New Jersey commented on Italian product innovation and potential for market extension.

> *After observing some of the Italian products, I find that the quality and innovativeness of them is only focused for the <u>Italian</u> consumer. Most of their products are only available and made for Italians. But I see no sign of innovation even remotely concerned with the rest of Europe and the world for that matter. These people are crazy not to capitalize upon the surrounding countries like France, Austria, and especially Switzerland. These*

places have more money to spend and all they need is a product which suits them.

Coming from Denmark, Jesper had somewhat different interests than the American students:

One of the things that surprised me the most... was that they are "like us" (the Danes). Before we came here most of us had the idea that Italy was a place where you could spend a vacation (a bit primitive), but as time passed we experienced a country that was much more sophisticated than we had expected.

One of the things that I found strange is the way Italian men dress. In Denmark, it would be "illegal" to wear a pink shirt unbuttoned to the belly button.

The women... are beautiful. They are well dressed, too, and a lot of them seem to be well-educated. We had some interesting bus rides, four blond boys in a bus... half the bus was staring at us and when you look one of them in the eyes, they keep staring.

Jennifer of Buffalo, New York had words of wisdom for the next crop of students:

1. *Jera will be your second mother whether you like it or not, but she is really cool.*
2. *(Re: Italian men)--take numbers, don't give them, or they will never stop calling.*
3. *Try everything once, you can always spit it out.*

Thomas, another Dane, shared his favorite Italian saying regarding the effects of bus strikes and opening hours: *"What we don't do today, we can always do tomorrow."*

Jennifer of Texas who was most often seen walking either Jera's dog, Aida, or her Italian boyfriend, Dario:

> *What I Have Learned: How to make tiramisu and gnocchi.*
> *Fashions Observed: cigarette pants & fishnet pantyhose.*
> *What I Have Found Out About Italian Men: They can make you fall in love.*

Amanda, an Iowa farm girl, had some interesting experiences, romantic and otherwise:

> *Italian drivers are too wild for me. I've seen three accidents, two involving mopeds, and one with a lady who was hit by a car and then got in the car with the guy who hit her.*
> *Before I came over here everyone was telling me, "Oh, you'll find a romantic Italian and get married." Well I have not found any romantic Italians. I've only found guys who think American women are easy. I'm not interested in Italian men because they are way too forward. I had a waiter who kissed me on my neck and asked if he could go home with me.*

Alessandra from Newcastle, California, most often seen in the company of Mark, told about her worst train experience: *Taking a train from Munich to Milan and waking up in Florence. I did not realize that the trains switch.*

Jill of Dayton, Ohio, was able to top Alessandra's worst train story and also related a frightening incident she witnessed at a soccer game:

On my way to Rome with Cassie and Jenn at 2:00 a.m. In Genoa the train conductor tells us our Eurail passes are no good and we have to get off and have the ticket office fix them. Not a problem right? It's Italy, don't forget. The conductor tells us that we have 5 minutes to find the ticket counter, explain the problem, and have them fix it. If we don't get it done within five minutes the train will leave without us. But here's the twist, only one of us can get off the train. We elected Jenn, and she did a good job and it only took her 4 minutes and 55 seconds!

Fondest Memory: At the calcio game with both Italians and Americans. When all of a sudden, an Italian fan throws a lit flare into the opposing teams bleachers. A small explosion results. Max, the native Italian next to me notices the look of horror on my face and says in a laughing voice, "Don't worry, everything is OK, that happens all the time." Now, nothing about Italy surprises me.

Karen from Oregon said her favorite part was that there's no drinking age, especially for those who are only 19: *Words of Wisdom To the Next Students: If you want to see some real Italian driving, tell your driver that you are in a hurry.*

Andrea who came from Idaho addressed the question as to which strike affected her most: *The bus strikes! By foot, it takes 45 minutes to get home.*

Henrik, another Dane, said his favorite food in Italy was the French Fries!

Another Andrea**,** this one Italian, gives some insight into his way of looking at things:

> *Favorite Italian Saying:* "We are 106 miles from Chicago, we have a full tank of gas, half packet of cigarettes, and we are both wearing sunglasses. HIT IT!!!!!!!!!!" P.S. Did you know that John Belushi and Dan Akroyd were Italian?????
>
> *Words of Wisdom to Next Students:* You don't need to throw spaghetti against the wall to see if they are cooked, just taste them!!!

In contrast to Mark, who said his fondest memories would be seeing Italy again through the eyes of new students here for the first time, I was more interested in seeing the world through the eyes of Italians, always wondering what they were thinking, what was their frame of reference, and what did they think of this crazy *straniero* trying to speak their language?

Italians are a curious and talkative people and it does not take much to generate interaction. Just saying *sono Americano* or *sono il professore visitando* would usually be enough to draw them out and start a conversation. The people who ran the shops and bars recognize you when you show up the second time and are patient enough to let you try out your Italian on them. Some will even say a few words in English in return. Of course, I was usually careful to give notice of my lack of fluency--"*non parlo bene l'italiano*"—-to which they would often counter, "Oh no, you speak very well!"

Geno who ran the Formaggio & Salumeria Deli is a case in point. His place was about two blocks from the apartment. I enjoyed stopping there once in awhile to take something home to eat. like anchovies or Bel Paese cheese or eggplant or crabmeat. And when I would enter Geno would expressively and good naturedly say, "Ah, Il Professore Pietro!" But I stopped going to Geno's deli after about 6 weeks. It had nothing to do with Geno. I simply lost my appetite for some of the food, especially the anchovies. Not because I no longer liked anchovies but because, like so many other things over there, they were so different from what I had been accustomed to. It was the whole fish, not just the filet, and had a very strong fishy taste. *"Il Professore,"* that's what he called me, intended as a warm and affectionate acknowledgment, I am sure. The feelings were mutual.

. . .

My favorite comment by one of the students was a double entendre from Ken who would later go to work for A.C. Nielson and Whitehall Labs after completing his degree program. It was one of those spontaneous, off-the-wall remarks that catches everyone, including the person who made it, by surprise. We were touring an old baroque palace near Torino called Stupinigi, when we came across a huge door that was hanging off its hinges in a part of the building yet to be renovated. It looked like something out of a haunted house. Ken said the door was "baroque." Get it?!

8

WHERE'S THE MINESTRONE?

What image of Italy did you have before you arrived? I thought the restaurants would have Italian food!

"I searched and I searched but I couldn't find..." Like the refrain of Crying in the Chapel, that hit song of the 1950's, no matter how hard I searched, there was no way on earth I was able to find... minestrone soup.

Many of my attempts to locate real Italian food in Italy were in vain. I *could* not find spaghetti and meatballs. I never encountered *bragiola* like grandma used to make. Believe it or not, I was unable to find pepperoni pizza until I discovered that over there they call it something else. And even then, it is totally different! I never saw any spumoni ice cream (although you wouldn't want it once you've tasted Italian *gelata,* which is richer and creamier). And as much as I searched and searched all over, rarely was I able to find minestrone soup!

Americans know minestrone as an Italian vegetable soup, often with pasta and beans tossed in. An Italian dictionary describes it simply as a thick vegetable soup. Popular variations include *minestrone alla Genovese* (with spinach, basil, and macaroni) and *minestrone verde* (with French beans and herbs). Progresso makes a nice canned minestrone in the States that's full of vegetables, beans, potatoes, and pasta. My grandma used to conjure up a soup she called *minestra* that contained spinach or escarole.

The authentic origins of minestrone, I am told, came from the peasant *contadina* families and the need to use up whatever leftovers happened to be available. Hence, the exact ingredients would vary from time to time and place to place.

One thing that does not vary, however, is the fact that minestrone is a staple of Italian cuisine, especially Italian-American cuisine. Any USA restaurant that calls itself "Italian" surely will have minestrone soup on the menu.

Yet, if you were to go to Italy today, you would not only *not* find minestrone, but you would also find yourself surrounded by lots of unfamiliar foods with strange sounding names. What to do? Right! You would try them, which is exactly what I did. For at least three days.

But, then you begin yearning for something familiar; something you *know* tastes good. Something you can trust. Something safe and secure like the feeling of being home again. Something like minestrone soup! Because you know that it is warm and hearty and can be trusted to provide a fulfilling meal. And it serves the same function as chicken soup in Jewish cuisine.

So, you would search. And when you don't find it, you'd ask someone: "What is going on here?" Which is precisely what I did! I asked Jera. At first she said, "You have to go to the South. Minestrone comes from the southern regions. You'll find it there." Later, she gave me still another excuse: "It's only October. You have to wait until the colder weather, then the restaurants will make your minestrone soup."

I didn't like her answers. After all, I looked around, scratched my head and said to myself, "This is Italy, isn't it? And Italian restaurants are supposed to have minestrone soup." So I took the discussion to Mark. "I'm going to write a book when I get back and I'm going to call it *Where's the Minestrone?*" He laughed and told me he thought it was a great title. And then we agreed that the food is totally different here.

So, how is it that so many people rave about it?

And *how* is it different?

Some foods simply go by different names, while others look and taste different. You won't find *mostaccioli, for example*—at least not by that name. They call it *penne* (a name also used in the USA), but it's the same thing. And anchovies, as I've already mentioned—yes, I am one of the half of one percent of the population who like anchovies. Waitresses in the States look at me like I am scum when I order them on my pizza. Now I am used to it. I just take it in stride and joke about it. Prosciutto and capocolla, the two most famous varieties of Italian ham. There is plenty of prosciutto in Italy, both *crudo* (raw) and *cotto* (cooked), but capocolla is not to be found!

Pizza, perhaps the most famous Italian food, is full of variations from what's found in the States. On one of my first visits to *Noe's* (Noah's) *Pizzeria,* a neighborhood hangout operated by an amiable Italian family, I ordered a *peperoni pizza*. But when they delivered it to the table, pepperoni was nowhere to be found! So, I beckoned to the *signora* to come look at my pizza.

"*Signora, dove il peperoni?*" I said, as I didn't see it on the pie and wanted to know where it was. She pointed to some green and red things and said, "*La* (There)." "No, no, this is not pepperoni!" But in Italy, it was. Peperoni is bell peppers, not sausage. Green and roasted and sweet, or simply marinated.

After I tried to explain what Americans mean when referring to pepperoni, her son brought out something that looked like an oversized hotdog or brat. I said "No, no, but *grazie* anyway." I later learned that if you want the sausage like our pepperoni, you order *salami picollo* or *pizza diavolo*—still not exactly the same thing.

Yes, pizza was full of variations. The black olives on pizza come whole and unpitted! An excellent taste treat, but hard on the teeth when you're not forewarned. Also popular: pizza with French fries on top, something my grandson, Tyler, thought was fascinating. And if there is such a thing as a national food among all the regionalisms of Italy, *Pizza Margherita* is it. Invented in 1889 as a tribute to Queen Margherita, wife of King Umberto, *Pizza Margherita* was designed as a patriotic expression of the green, white, and red colors of the flag of the newly unified Italy. Made with olive oil, basil leaves (the green), cheese (the white), and tomatoes (the red), it still is one of the more popular variations of pizza in Italy today. So is *Quattro Stagione*, meaning Four Seasons, a tantalizing pizza with each quarter containing a different variety of ingredients. A great idea that some American pizza chains have made a poor attempt at imitating!

I looked for *Scamorza*, or smoked *scamorza*—a rubbery cheese my family used to buy in Cincinnati. It is an aged *mozzarella* only firmer and saltier. In Italy, I never saw it on any of the hundreds of plates of food that I consumed. Nor did I see it on any of the restaurant menus. Mark says I should have looked for it in the markets.

• • •

Gloria thought the main difference between Italian and Italian-American food was the sauces—"They're heavy," she said, "and they cook with lots of seafood." Gloria doesn't like seafood and she was sometimes afraid to order spaghetti with tomato sauce because she firmly believed there would be some seafood lurking in the sauce.

With all that sauce, some bread might be just the thing, right? To tell you the truth, I was not crazy about the Italian bread. Now I must admit I'm not a big bread eater to begin with. But Gloria is, and she wasn't thrilled with it, either. Of course, Mark says the bread is wonderful.

There are basically two kinds of bread in Italy. First are the *Grossini* bread sticks that are straw-shaped, about eight to ten inches long, and have a texture more like crackers than bread. Wrapped two or more to a package, they appear on tables in eating establishments almost everywhere. I saw them in snack bars, restaurants, in the lunchroom of the school. I saw them in the North and in the South. They are okay to eat if you have no other choice but they don't even look Italian. It would be interesting to find out how these things got into the country in the first place.

The other kind of bread looks exactly like you would expect Italian bread to look. But it is hard. Now, sometimes I enjoy a piece of bread when it is hot, moist, and flavorful, like Mama Bella hot garlic bread. But not when it is cold, dry, and hard. In all fairness to the Italian bread makers, I must confess that everyone else, other than Gloria and me, seemed to love the bread. Maybe they have teeth made of steel, I don't know.

Breakfast is another good example of how eating in Italy is different. Italians don't eat breakfast. Standard fare includes a *briosche* (a sweet pastry) with cappuccino. Maybe cereal and/or a fruit. Prunes is also a favorite breakfast item they feed to the tourists in all the hotels. Sadly (or fortunately, perhaps), you don't see the kinds of choices that Americans take for granted, like bacon and eggs, pancakes and waffles. No home fries, biscuits and gravy, or grits. Toast bread—rarely. At best, you'll have a choice of hard Italian rolls, *briosche* or crackers. Go for the *briosche*, especially if they are hot out of the oven. Now they *are* wonderful!

Some things that have popped up in the States in recent years are supposedly Italian, but I did not see them in Italy. Bread dipped in olive oil, for example: increasingly popular over here but in Italy...never saw it! And the wineglasses in some of the nouveau Italian-American restaurants that look like small juice glasses? In Italy, we never saw them. They use stems, even for water.

. . .

Italy accommodates other ethnic restaurants, including American-style fast-food places, Mexican, and Chinese. In *Torino*, for example, there is a McDonald's, a local McDonald's look-alike, a couple of Mexican/Spanish restaurants, and more than a couple of Chinese (*Cinese*) restaurants.

One evening I went to a Chinese restaurant since the search for minestrone was not going well. I got really excited about having a bowl of good old reliable, safe and secure hot and sour soup. Nope! The Chinese restaurants there don't have it and, furthermore, they act like they never heard of it!

. . .

Like the restaurants and the food, the Italian bars are quite different. They are not like American bars although here and there you will find a few that pretend to be, and even call themselves "American Bar." The disguise is usually so transparent it is rather like a rabbit carrying a sign that says "turtle!"

Bars are sometimes called *il bar*, sometimes *il caffe*, or sometimes they are part of a dining establishment and may be called something else. Small in size, they look more like an ice-cream parlor or coffee shop, although they serve beer, wine, and liquor as well as espresso, cappuccino, and sandwiches (*panini*). I think this is due to the fact that Italians don't 'drink.' At a downtown festa, for example, everybody was eating gelato (ice-cream); nobody was in the bars drinking. They were walking up and down the streets eating ice cream!

Unlike in American bars, you don't see bar stools, mood lighting, or jukeboxes. Customers either stand at the counter, sit at one of the few small tables inside, or sit at a table outside, weather permitting. Music usually comes from a radio behind the bar or in the kitchen. Lighting is almost always bright, a remarkable contrast to the 15-watt bulbs burning in the apartment. On the shelf behind the bar, you're likely to see an array of strange-looking bottles, mainly aperitifs, liqueurs, scotches and wines, in brands I did not recognize. Very little in the way of bourbons or blends, although I did notice a fifth of Jack Daniel's or Four Roses on occasion.

One time I asked for a Seven-Seven, a concoction of Seagram's 7-Crown, Seven-Up, and a twist of lemon. At least, that's the way my dad always made it. For years it was his favorite drink, and later mine.

The server was dumbfounded. She was a young Italian woman who spoke bits and pieces of English, and was trying really hard to understand. I knew they had the ingredients (J. Daniel's, not Seagram's), so I explained how to make one and she said they can't do that! I said, "Si, si, you can do it"--and I explained again, partly in Italian. Well, here is how she did it. First, she brought a glass half-filled with JD (no ice yet), and an unopened can of Sprite. Then, she came back ten minutes later with a small bowl of ice and put two tiny ice cubes in my glass, and that was it! But, that was fine! I

> *enjoyed it anyway. She must have felt sorry for me because at the end of the meal she surprised me with free ice-cream for dessert!*

. . .

When I finally got to travel south to Rome, Bellona, Caserta, Sorrento, and other towns in the vicinity of Naples, I still did not find much in the way of familiar Italian food. But I must admit the food there was much more to my liking! I had been led to believe that there would be significant differences from North to South, and I'm sure there are, but to the untrained eye, the differences seemed mostly minor, especially at first.

By late October, not only was I searching the South for that elusive bowl of minestrone, but for Carusone family roots as well. I even made it to my dad's hometown of Bellona for the greater part of a day. But, when all was said and done, I found neither familiar foods nor family that I could identify as being directly related, though I did meet several Carusones. Hey, I had a good time, met some nice people, and enjoyed some wonderful food for a change, even though it was still not quite what I had been accustomed to back home.

In Caserta, for example, I had dinner at a place called `Soletti,` recommended by an Italian businessman I met on the train from Rome to Naples. He and the guy he was talking with had caught my attention because their conversation was so animated and expressive. The gestures they were making indicated that they were talking from the stomach, with hands cupped loosely together but churning constantly in an upward and outward rotation. I was told to go to `Soletti's` and "ask for `Franco,`" which I did, and that "the food will be wonderful," which it was! I ordered Buffalo cheese and a pizza.

Ah! Real Neapolitan pizza made with olive oil, tomatoes, and oregano—and no cheese. Remember, Naples is where pizza originated. In fact, *Pizza marinara*—with olive oil, tomatoes, oregano, and garlic—first appeared in Naples around 1760, if you can believe that! I asked the waiter to add one other important ingredient—*carciofi* (artichoke hearts). This was the best pizza I had the whole time I was in Italy! By far!

As for Buffalo cheese, it is a form of mozzarella I had not heard of before. Up and down the streets of Caserta there are store signs hanging all over for *"Mozzarella di Bufalo"* (pronounced BOO'-FAH-LOW), apparently a local specialty. They say you must eat it fresh, before it is more than 24 hours old! I tried it as an appetizer. It came as a self-contained ball of about four inches in diameter, which is a lot of cheese for one person. It was so fresh that when I cut into it, juices actually squirted out! The texture was a tad rubbery but it tasted very good.

I had another wonderful meal in Caserta—in the dining room of the Jolly hotel where I was staying. The first surprise was that the bartender actually knew how to make a Manhattan. And it was a great one, with a nice twist—a rind of lemon. Then I was served an *arugala* salad with tiny shrimp and fresh sliced cherry tomatoes in a dressing of olive oil and lemon juice with spices. Mmmmmm, it was so good. This is something I will try to recreate one of these days as my mouth waters just thinking about it.

The Jolly Hotel is great for any travelers who have had their fill of the inconveniences that so often accompany typical foreign accommodations. If you want to be spoiled with a touch of class and comfort, for a price, you can depend on the Jolly for consistently top-notch accommodations, amenities, and great service. Gloria and I had dinner one evening at the Jolly in Torino (the hotel is an upscale chain with locations in many Italian cities and some other European countries) and it, too, was a wonderful experience. No, unfortunately, I am neither being paid nor given any perks by the Jolly people in exchange for this valuable promotional plug. However, if they wish to show their undying gratitude after the fact—which they should!—by offering to me and my extended family of 25 a week's free stay at one of their prime locations, hey, I am not one to look a gift horse in the mouth!

· · ·

I traveled a lot in October: Rome, then Locarno, Switzerland (on a lake), then Florence. In Rome, I really got lucky when I discovered *the Derby Ristorante*, an elegant, intimate place with a capable and accommodating staff. They are not paying me to say this but I think they should.

The Derby is in the Embassy district off Via Veneto. I was attracted by their ad in a tourist brochure listing a piano bar and disco in the lounge of the restaurant. I still had not found the traditional Italian music and dancing I was looking for, so, I called and made reservations.

The walk from the nearest subway station at the bottom of Via Veneto took about 40 minutes, much of it uphill. I thought I would never get there. On the way I passed the U.S. Embassy. By the time I finally arrived, my body felt like it was ready for a special treat, and a treat it was.

The dinner at the Derby that night was rather simple: a wonderful shrimp and avocado appetizer, and a succulent peppercorn filet mignon. I opted to bypass the *primo piatto*. The avocado was cut in the shape of little round balls, almost like marbles, and it came with a nice white sauce. The steak was like heaven— I had been avoiding meats since an early experience with fatty sausage at the school. This was the first time I felt safe about ordering steak since arriving in Italy. I enjoyed this dinner so much that I would return weeks later with Gloria on my second trip to Rome.

After the meal, I was escorted to the disco lounge where two piano players—a father and son team—were alternating at the piano. The place was packed and really jamming but they found a spot for me right on the side of the piano. The songs were upbeat modern versions of Italian music—not traditional but very enjoyable, nonetheless. No one sang *Oh Solo Mio*, or *Oh, Marie*. There was, however, one song where the word *Americano* would pop up in the refrain and the piano player, eyes gleaming, would look at me and smile. That made me feel good. Maybe I was the token *Americano* for the evening? In fact, I often had the feeling that Italians consider it good luck to have an American patronizing their place of business, and not just because of the money we spend.

The experience at the Derby was a far cry from my entertainment of the night before. In my continuing search for "traditional entertainment," I literally uncovered a secret hideaway, a place I learned about earlier in the day talking with servers at a bar in *Campo de' Fiori*. I had asked them where one could go for some good Italian entertainment, and they wrote the name and address of this place on a piece of paper and gave it to me. In retrospect, maybe it was their idea of a joke.

To get to the club, I had to take a cab, as the night club was tucked away in the rear of a small apartment building in the middle of an obscure residential section of the city. By all indications, the taxi driver was not familiar with this part of town. He drove up and down several no-outlet streets in search of the address, all the while talking to himself in a frustrating tone of voice.

It was about 10:00 p.m. when the cab dropped me off. I walked cautiously around to the rear of the building, all too aware of what a dumb thing I was doing. Just being there, on a dark street in a desolate neighborhood of a strange city in a foreign country, alone. Now, that was a dumb thing to do.

Sure enough, around back there was a door with the name of the club on it but the doorman did not want to let me in. I could hear voices inside and much scurrying about. The people in charge wanted to know my identity and how I came to know about the place. Well, that made me even more curious and determined to get in.

They said the doors would not open until after 11:00 o'clock (*l'undici*), and the entertainment would not begin until midnight. I said fine (*va bene*). I stood around outside waiting patiently, walked around the grounds a short distance, and at eleven I engaged the managers in conversation once again to see if they would now let me in. I told them I had come all the way from America for some good Italian entertainment. Well, after some further delay and more arguing, they finally relented and let me in. The place was virtually empty. A hostess seated me at a small table and served me a drink. Everyone was polite but they still seemed to be regarding me with suspicion.

By the time the entertainment got started, I had had a couple of drinks and was thinking about leaving already. They had singers and comedy routines that were enjoyable to watch but not what you would call traditional. Since the comedy was all in Italian and fast-paced, I couldn't understand most of it. At about 1:30 I asked someone to call me a taxi. I never did figure out what was so secretive or so special about the place, or why they were reluctant to let me in.

· · ·

By the time I departed Italy I had tried many different foods. Some I actually liked, and a few I even got excited about. My favorites would have to include the *Penne Pasta Arrabiata* at Noe's Pizzeria and the *brezaola,* a dried salted beef, especially nice as an appetizer sliced thin and sprinkled with olive oil and lemon juice. Popular side dishes *(contorni)* that would keep me coming back were *patate fritte* (deep fried potatoes), *piselli* (peas), and *spinaci* (spinach). The Torrone I had in Alba, and the fresh chestnuts roasted on an open fire, I knew my mother would like!

As anyone who calls himself an Italian-American would surely know, Torrone is a traditional Italian candy. It's an oblong nougat about two inches by one inch, wrapped in foil and packaged singly inside cute little boxes. Its texture is chewy, contains nuts, and it comes in flavors like vanilla, orange, and lemon. A special holiday treat, it is often served in homes on Easter Sunday. The Torrone at the festa in Alba were in a bulk form I had not seen before, big chunks about a foot long and wider than the ones that come in a box. They were being sold by the pound.

I decided to try something new at the festa in Alba— truffles. Not the chocolate truffles mind you, but the fungus-like stuff that grows at the base of certain trees that dogs and pigs are used to help ferret.

These truffles are a real delicacy and are very expensive. After paying an extra $7.00 for truffle shavings on top of my ravioli, I found them to be disappointing. They smelled like perfume to me and had a rather odd, indescribable taste. Pigs are said to like them because they emit a steroid similar to a pheromone produced by boars' pre-mating behavior. I think one must develop an acquired taste for truffles and at seven dollars an ounce I did not feel strongly motivated to do so.

My friend, Professor Bob, had his own experience with truffles:

> *Ciao Pete*
> *Just got back from the truffle fair in Alba. Can't believe that people will pay that much for something that looks and smells*

> *that bad. The first marketing exec for the truffle finders group must have been some brilliant individual. I did sample some of the sauces, cheeses, and meats and figured that we really didn't need to develop a taste for the fungus.*

And what about the minestrone? Did I ever find it? Actually, I did. On a Sunday afternoon about two months into the trip, I was between trains in Bologna, with ample time for walking around the district near *la stazione*. The fact that this happened on a Sunday is significant because, remember, just about everything in Italy was closed on Sundays. Consequently, you can understand my delight at finding that in Bologna there actually were shops and restaurants open, as was also the case in tourist-oriented Pisa.

Across the street from the station music was playing and people were selling CDs and cassettes from tables on the sidewalk. I bought an audio cassette from a street vendor and continued on my little mini-tour. I meandered into a courtyard area with more shops when, lo and behold, there it was before me—a sign in the window of a *ristorante* that said "MINESTRONE!" I couldn't believe my eyes.

I went in and seated myself and waited. My mouth watering in anticipation, it seems like I waited for a very long time, though it was probably only eight or ten minutes. Then, finally, the waitress came over to my table. I remember saying to her in my best Italian, "*Minestrone, per favore.*" I could almost taste it, at long last, my elusive minestrone soup. The waitress looked at me and nonchalantly let me know that they were out of it. Just like that!

So, I walked out and strolled around the other side of the courtyard area, disappointed of course but more hopeful than before. Then, unbelievably, there was yet another place with a sign in the window advertising minestrone soup. And this time it was for real. They were not out of it! I ordered and was served my wonderful bowl of minestrone and I enjoyed every drop of it! Not great, but very good, and certainly fulfilling in more ways than one.

. . .

There will be more to say about the food in Italy in Chapter 13 (*What? You Don't Like the Food?!*) and Chapter 18 (*"Meatballs, Mischief & Miscellany"*). So as we conclude this chapter on minestrone, permit me to give you some brotherly advice. It is this: Although the food is different, if you are brave enough to try enough strange-looking stuff with names you don't recognize, eventually you will find something you'll really like. It just so happens that most of the yummy dishes I discovered were to be found in the southern part of the country, although the people of the North may not be readily appreciative of such an assessment.

An interesting point of culinary comparison between North and South is the *Napolitano* pizza I have already talked about. This is the one I found in Caserta, the one that was the absolute best. I liked it so much that I wanted one like it after returning to Torino. However, getting the *Torinese* to make me the same pizza as the one I enjoyed near Naples was not in the cards:

> *Tried to order (HERE IN TORINO) a real Napolitano pizza the other night (olive oil, tomatoes, oregano, no cheese) like I had when I was in Caserta but they didn't think it sounded good so I wound up with something else. It's a reverse twist of customer orientation—they don't care what you really want, they want to give you what THEY think tastes good! What they think you*

should have. So, I wound up with a pizza all right—with tomatoes, potatoes, mozzarella, funghi—and twigs.

9

NON C'E' MALE

Come sta? (How are you?) you might be asked. To which you would aptly respond by saying *bene* (fine), or *cosi cosi* (so so), or *non c'e' male* (not bad).

For some reason unbeknownst to me, I happened to notice that when Italians respond to *"Come sta?"* (pronounced COH-MAY-STAH'), most of the time the answer is *non c'e' male* (NAWN-CHAY-MAH'-LAY)! Maybe I'm making a big deal about nothing, but this seemed to me indicative of something interesting about the Italian mentality. Italian attitudes. Something worth further analysis.

Now, you have to understand that it is virtually impossible to get inside the Italian psyche. No matter how friendly the people may be, it is like there is an invisible shield you cannot penetrate. Some would say that this is typical of more formal cultures in general, not just Italy, but in countries like Germany, France, Great Britain, and Japan as well. I think it also has something to do with the concept of paradox and contradiction alluded to in earlier chapters, and with the notion of inside versus outside. And I believe it is related as well to the concept of "Fortress Mentality," which I'll get to in the next chapter. Essentially, it is like there is a public face and a very private face behind every Italian persona. What you see is not necessarily what you get!

Sadie Penzato in her book about *Growing Up Sicilian and Female* cites a Sicilian proverb: *"Don't spit at heaven, it will fall in your face."* She says Sicilians believe that if you brag about something or become too proud of your possessions or loved ones, you "tempt the Gods" and misfortune will befall you.

If you say *non c'e' male*, what you mean is "not good but not bad." It is an understatement. It's like saying "Hey, I am not going to tell you that I'm doing great because that would be asking for trouble." It would be a jinx. In fact, if you think I'm well off, you might even want me to help you in some way. After all, the last shall be first and the first shall be last, right? So, why stick my neck out? Besides, when you present yourself in a low-key, understated way, people don't expect too much. Then, it becomes easier to make a good impression when they see you doing a good job. At international business meetings, for example, the Italians are known to arrive late, appear disorganized and with chaos surrounding them but, invariably, turn around and do a surprisingly outstanding job! Bravo!

Another interesting aspect of this tendency toward understatement, paradox, and contradiction shows up at the national level in Italy's political and economic track record. On the one hand, you have government bureaucracy, heavy taxation, and other legal and political obstacles. Since 1945 Italy has had about 45 governments, not an easy environment in which to operate a business.

On the other hand, look at what's been achieved! Italy is one of the G-7 nations, a political power on the world scene, a member of NATO, and a founding member of the European Community. It boasts a national income that ranks consistently among the top 10 of the largest economies in the world! How a country with one hand tied behind its back is able to achieve such high economic status is certainly an enigma.

Maybe the *non c'e' male* syndrome has to do with a kind of martyr complex and the notion of struggle. After all, people often perform better under pressure—for example, "Look at how much I am hurting but I go on anyway."

When Gloria and I were in Saint Vincent, in the beautiful bilingual Aosta region north of Torino, an elderly gentleman who walked with a limp—after being asked for directions—-made a valiant effort to guide us to the train station. Not just point the way but actually take us there!

The sun had just gone down and it was starting to get cold. We followed as he led us along the dark road with no sidewalks, up and down the hills. He kept complaining about his leg. I told him that I was sure we could find it now, and thanked him for his trouble. But he kept walking, limping, and complaining! He would not stop and he would not listen to my pleas. He just kept walking and complaining. Finally, with the train station clearly in sight, he bid us farewell, and would not even let us give him anything for his trouble.

• • •

Cell phones. Hi-tech cell phones everywhere! Certainly not an understated posture as in "not good, not bad." I think Mark was right—-it's a status thing—big time! Even more so than in the states, and a good two years before it hit the USA. Walking or driving down the street. On the trains and buses, *"Ciao!"* In bars and restaurants, people take their seats, placing cell phone in full view on the table. "B*rrrriiiiing!* *"Ciao! Come sta?"*

I would imagine that for some this new preoccupation may be a real irritant, aside from the obvious hazard of phoning while driving. Flooding the air with private conversation to which others listen but pretend not to. Taking one's attention away from those close at hand. For example, the attractive young couple seated next to me in a nice *ristorante* on a Saturday evening--the woman talked on the phone for a good *20 minuti* while her escort sat there cooling his heels. Amazing!

. . .

Piazzas everywhere. They are wonderful, of course! A piazza is just a public square, often anchored by a church or some other famous landmark. Like the Egyptian obelisk to the side of the *Piazza San Giovanni in Laterano*, in Rome. Piazzas are used for festas, open-air markets, or just for people walking and hanging around. Piazzas are like open green spaces, but without the green.

Italians like to walk. They walk everywhere. I never walked so much in my life! The *passagiata*—it is neat to see, hundreds walking, couples arm-in-arm, leisurely strolling and enjoying the cool evening air. Some streets are totally blocked off to vehicular traffic for the evening hours, or for a special festa like the 10-day event in downtown Torino to celebrate the launching of the new Fiat models, Bravo and Brava. Blocking off traffic to allow pedestrians the luxury of having the whole street for walking is a great idea. We could learn from them.

. . .

Soccer, soccer, and more soccer. Sports is often a topic of conversatiion in our family. While keeping in touch and checking on the grandkids, the subject matter inevitably turns to sports.

Went to a bar with Charles, Piegeorgio (the father of the family he lives with), and Silvio (the son) to see the Milan/Rome soccer match.

Tell Tyler to keep up the good work on his football team (52-18, Wow!). Is Nick playing soccer or football? All they care about over here is soccer, of course, called calcio (like CAL-CHO).

I was amazed to see how completely the Italians, like Europeans in general, are consumed by soccer. I mean, I knew about this before the trip, but the focus and intensity surprised me. Everywhere people talked about the 'big game,' watched it on the tube if they couldn't actually be there, and let their emotions go crazy in public places, even engaging in riotous behavior on occasion. What also surprised me was their lack of interest in other sports. For example, no news coverage whatsoever of American baseball. Okay, I can understand that since they think baseball is weird. But, the World Series? Nothing, not in the local press or on CNN International! Granted, they don't give a hoot about baseball, but after all, this is the WORLD series, right?!

Actually, there is considerable interest in NBA basketball in Italy. But as for American football or baseball—zilch!

. . .

Domestic women. Feminists would have a field day in *Italia*! The role of women in society has not changed much from the old days, even in the big cities. The percentage of women in the Italian labor force in the late 1990s was the same as in 1960, and the lowest in Europe! For those employed outside the home, that work just gets added to all the domestic stuff they still have to do! Now I understand what he meant when the British novelist, E. M. Forster, wrote in 1905 that "Italy is such a delightful place to live in if you happen to be a man."

Well, I thought I would have a little fun with this in a fax I sent back home about the advantages of being male in Italian society.

> *One of the neat things about Italy is how they keep the wives home and make them wash and cook and clean all the time. Meals are always on the table promptly. The men do not lift a finger around the house! Women like Jera (the program director at the school) who work outside the home are considered to be feminist extremists.*
>
> *My friend Charles lives with an Italian family and the mother does everything for him. She does laundry everyday. He folded his socks himself once, and she came along and refolded them! Maybe I will make some changes in the Carusone household when I return?! (Just joking, Gloria, just joking.)*

. . .

Foreign women. "They are easy" seems to be the predominant attitude of Italian males. I observed this attitude myself on more than one occasion. I heard about it from some of the American female students. And I heard about it from Jera.

Of course, it is indisputable that one of the reasons why some women go to Italy in the first place is, well, to find a romantic experience, shall we say. I believe that. I saw two women from Poland pick up an Italian waiter. He told me, "The Polish... they are easy."

. . .

"*Bravo!*" That's what I heard when Gloria and I exited the bus. It made me feel like a hero, though later I would discover the meaning of the word *bravo,* which is *clever* and not *brave* as I had thought. It was my only brush with the law—well, not really the law but rather those affectionately known in bus rider circles as the Ticket Gestapo.

You see, for Italians the week begins on Monday, not on Sunday as in our calendar. What does that have to do with anything, you say? Just this. When you buy a *settimanale* (weekly) bus pass, it is good for the week beginning on a Monday and ending on a Sunday. You must validate the pass the first time you use it by inserting it into a stamping machine on the bus. Well, I was stamping mine every week on a Sunday, which technically made it invalid the next day because Sunday belongs to the previous week and not the following week!

It happened one day when Gloria and I were taking the bus to school. Lo and behold, this guy walks down the aisle, pulls out a badge, slaps it on his coat and announces that he is going to check tickets. When he saw that mine was stamped on Sunday, he said it was invalid. Well, I argued with him—in my best Italian—that I was a foreigner ("*Sono straniero!*") and that I thought the week began on Sunday. Otherwise, I pointed out, why would I stamp it on the very last day of the week? That wouldn't make any sense, would it?

The more animated and vocal I became, the more this guy began to back off. Then he finally gave up on me and decided to move on. When Gloria and I got off the bus a couple of stops later, a middle-aged man also exiting looked at me and spoke one word: "*Bravo!*" Apparently, he had enjoyed seeing how I stood up to the authorities and won, and he thought I was clever. I felt like Robin Hood!

I think the incident was indicative of a larger phenomenon, namely, the docility of Italians and, to some extent, Europeans in general, especially when compared with Americans. It is one of those things we take for granted in this great country of ours—an individual sense of empowerment. The idea that we—any of us—can change a situation. We can do something about it. We don't have to blindly accept what some muckity-muck official says. Of course, if we had police walking around carrying little machine guns all the time, maybe we would be more docile, too?!

Despite this theory of "docility," I think Italian people have an intense sense of curiosity. Or maybe they are just plain nosey! It seems they are always checking you out as you're walking down the street, or standing on the corner. Very discreetly, of course. You get the feeling they are all participating in some grandiose neighborhood watch. It is like they are looking you over, often taking an almost excessive interest in whatever it is you happen to be doing.

. . .

A lot like Cheers, where everybody knows your name. In my next life I think I would like to spend it just hanging out at an Italian bar. The various characters who populate the Italian bar scene are fascinating. Some of the regulars are in and out several times throughout the day, staying perhaps for no more than five or ten minutes. Some stand around for hours, acting like they own the place, looking like they're waiting for something important to happen. Others appear to be taking part in a kind of melodrama complete with operatic intonations and theatrical gestures. It is not unusual for the proprietor to be delivering cappuccino or espresso on a tray to customers up and down the street at the neighboring establishments.

There is a bar on Via Guala where I occasionally stopped on the way from school to sit and have a beer. It is located across the street from a camera shop. Every evening at about 6:00 P.M. the bespectacled owner of the camera shop, dressed in a white laboratory jacket, would lock his door, put a sign in the window, scurry across the street, and have a quick aperitif. It was funny the way he would rush in and rush out, with only a minimal exchange of words, without a smile, and in such a formal manner.

I had read years ago about the popular practice of *adopting* a bar in Italy. Maybe adopting is not the right word. It is more than your favorite, usual neighborhood bar hangout. It is more like a second home. It is a forum, a refuge, a security blanket. It is important to bond with this bar. Not to be confused, of course, with the drinking places where barflies hang out in the USA, and where the prime activity is consuming alcohol and often getting inebriated—unlike what I observed earlier about the differences between American and Italian bars, and the fact that Italians rarely get drunk.

Simply put, the Italian bar is a center of social activity. It is a place where you can feel at home, have something refreshing to drink and eat, and visit with familiar faces. Well, I was constantly on the lookout for such a bar that would be a good match for me. I thought I had found it in a place called "Billy Bar."

When I first walked into Billy Bar I had a good feeling about the place. I began to stop by two or three times a week, in the morning for cappuccino or on the way home for espresso or *birra (beer)*. Billy Bar was run by an amicable man by the name of Maurizio who reminded me a lot of my uncle Tom—smiling and joking a lot with the customers. Maurizio had been to Utah and Vegas and liked to try out his English on me. He seemed like a happy person, at least the first few times I saw him.

One morning I stopped by and Maurizio was not there. I got to meet Lena, an outgoing, cordial woman working the bar along with Maurizio's brother, Antonio. (Let me tell you, there are more Antonio's in Italy than anything!) Antonio, too, was nice and easygoing, So far, so good. I thought I had found the bar I was looking for, and now knew three people there: Maurizio, Lena, and Antonio.

Over time, though, I began to notice an abrupt change in Maurizio's attitude and disposition. He was suddenly projecting a very serious, even sour, side of his personality. Had something tragic happened in his life to change him, or was it something about me? I never learned the answer. When you only know a smattering of the language, it limits your ability to probe and understand.

The last time I stopped at Billy Bar I was served a briosche that was so stale it must have been at least two days old! Inexcusable in *Italia*! I never returned.

. . .

The News. An Italian newspaper reported the outrage of actress Brigitte Nielsen because an Arab sheik offered to pay her a million dollars if she would spend the night with him. The story received quite an interesting reaction. The headline of the story read *Brigitte Nielsen: io non mi vendo,* which literally means "I do not sell myself." Nielsen was quoted as saying:

> "I wouldn't make love to a stranger, not even for ten million dollars. I have never had sex for money. I'm not capable of it."

The reaction in Italy, especially from some of the Italian film starlets, was quite remarkable, and speaks volumes about Italian attitudes toward sexuality. Actress Natalia Estrada was quoted as saying: *"If he had only asked me, but unfortunately you know how Arabs are, they prefer blondes. It might have been fun, a fairy tale weekend spent on a yacht."*

Gabriella Carlucci implied that she would not be scandalized by such an offer. *"Arab men still have a strong sense of gallantry. If I were not happily married..."*

Nielsen, who has appeared in some 25 films including *Rocky IV,* has been married five times.

. . .

Shopping. Shopping in Italy is such a delight! Even if you don't like to shop, you will enjoy it, believe me. There are so many interesting little shops, and very few of the boring modern cookie-cutter stores and shopping centers like we have.

Of course, the first enclosed shopping mall in the world, the *Galleria,* is to be found right in downtown Milan's city streets and boasts a canopy. Built in the late 19th century, the *Galleria* is still a beehive of activity. There is a large seal on the ground—very much like a zodiac sign, perhaps Taurus, perhaps a reference to the story of Jupiter and the white bull— where you are supposed to stand and whirl yourself around for good luck. We saw people of all ages and descriptions having fun performing this ritual.

I was told that Americans go shopping to shop, and stop to eat only incidentally; while Italians go to the shopping district downtown to eat, and then shop as a secondary activity. Italians dine to socialize, not to eat. That's why it takes them so long. Also, they eat very little of each course, and enjoy the wine, always taking their time. Since I am a very slow eater, like my mother, I can appreciate the meals that consume three and four hours. For me it is almost like nonstop eating as one meal overlaps with the next!

One of my most memorable social experiences was an Italian dinner party at the home of Graziana, a friend of Jera. Graziana graciously provides accommodations for exchange students at the school, and even for a visiting scientist when needed.

Graziana hosted the typical upper-class dinner party for eight. One of the guests, an American scientist (very

New Yorkish), had a theory about a new way to go to the moon! What a character this guy was. A cross between Danny DeVito and Columbo!

At first I thought the guy was blowing smoke—a new way to go to the moon! C'mon! "Do you mean a new form of transport, or a new trajectory, or what?" I asked. He said it was a new path that would save time. He was visiting for a three-week consultation with Alenia, the Italian aircraft company.

This man was a scientist?

And there was more. Instead of continuing to socialize after he ate, the scientist instead left immediately to go play ping-pong! No social graces whatsoever. Didn't he know that it's not polite to eat and run, especially in Italy where the dinner conversation goes on and on? Especially when the dinner is in your honor!

The hostess was livid. So of course all the guests talked about "Mr. Genius" and his lack of social skills. Everyone else was afraid to leave for fear the others would then talk about them! Very colorful.

During the coming weeks, I would hear more stories about this man's bizarre behavior. Like when he opened the front-load washing machine while it was still cycling and dumped water all over the floor—he'd thought it was a dishwasher. And, we learned, he washed his hair with dog shampoo. I guess that's happens when you go to another country without taking the time to learn the language.

. . .

La Vita Americano. It is not easy to characterize Italian attitudes toward America. Do they love us? Do they hate us? Do they think we are all *pazzo* (crazy)?

I saw many signs of *Americana* in Italy, beginning with the very popular McDonald's in downtown Torino and advertisements for a Holiday on Ice show. I saw billboards proclaiming "Buon Compleano (Happy Birthday) to Topo

Gigio," the little Italian mouse cartoon character popular in the States when I was a boy. Yes, Topo Gigio is still alive and well in *Italia*! I also saw a sign saying "Buon Compleano, Elvis!" And a Jack Daniels cap on display in the window of a small shop.

I do know there is a belief that America is *troppo esagerato*, that we are overly exaggerated and over reactive with respect to issues like smoking, wearing seat belts, and other safety and health concerns. They think we go to extremes and have a tendency to make a mountain out of a molehill.

. . .

Inside versus outside. Other observers of the Italian scene have documented an amazing contrast between the outside appearance of Italian homes and the inside. At Graziana's, for example, the exterior of the building housing her apartment looked like just another scruffy old building. But behind the locked and bolted exterior doors was a charming courtyard with a nice assortment of shrubs and flowers, and inside a very nicely appointed apartment.

Despite the fact that nearly every apartment has its own balcony, you never see people out on them except when they are hanging clothes or thrashing a rug. I wondered what was going on here. Why aren't the Italians sitting on their balconies?

I asked Andrea, an Italian student who was working in the USAC office. He said people don't sit out on their balconies because "they don't want to show themselves." Maybe it has to do with a sense of privacy, or the distinction between the public face and the private face.

. . .

Familia. I met another Peter Carusone. Here is how it happened.

As soon as I arrived in Bellona, I started asking people if they knew the Carusones. I stopped in a bar for a draft beer (*birra spina*) and I said, "*Conosce Lei la familia Carusone?*" And they asked *which* Carusone and on what street they lived. Of course I had no idea. I talked to an old man leaning against the iron fence in front of his house situated high up off the street. *Conosce Lei la familia Carusone?* I explained that my grandfather had left for America some 70 years ago—as if it were something that happened yesterday. Seventy years ago! He smiled and pointed this way, then that way, but 70 years is a long time.

I stopped and talked with two young girls sitting in front of a house, one holding a baby. *Conosce Lei la familia Carusone?* They told me to wait there. A few minutes later a man in his 60s came out who said his mother was a Carusone. Aha!

The man was amicable and talkative. We sat on the stoop and chatted for awhile. His English was more than passable. He had spent years abroad, mainly in Australia. He proudly showed me some of the improvements he had done to the old house.

Then he invited me inside where an elderly woman had a big pile of greens cooking in this little bitty pot on the stove. The greens must have been stacked about six inches higher than the top of the pot. Next to the stove was a big TV set. We talked some more. The man brought out a phone book and showed me there were 20 to 25 Carusones in the book, including four Pietros! He called one on the phone and asked him to come over to meet me. About a half-hour later, Pietro Carusone arrived. About 35 years old, he was nice looking and quite casual in his demeanor. We were introduced, and we sat there and barely communicated. He spoke no English. He seemed disinterested. We never connected.

. . .

Attention to detail. Maybe the reason why Italians have produced so many great artists, craftsmen, and designers of world renown is due to their attention to detail. They are fastidious and like things a certain way. Look at the shoes and designer fashions. Look at the buildings. Look at the presentation of the food—it is out of this world! Cappuccino with a flower, or your initials, on top. Candy and pastries as beautifully wrapped as any regal gift. I once saw a man operating a street-sweeping vehicle who stopped and got out to pick up a single piece of paper that the brushes missed.

. . .

I discovered a lot about Italian attitudes on my first visit to Italy. I learned that there are two kinds of people in this world—givers and takers. Italians, for the most part, are givers. But sometimes you have to ask.

10

WHAT'S YOUR HAND DOING IN MY POCKET?

An Italian TV station once staged a pickpocket championship for nimble-fingered youth. A good laugh, unless it's your pocket that's being picked.

The bus was packed and I was among the standing, as usual. I don't mind standing because it gives you a better view of where you are and more time to anticipate your destination. This is important when you're in a strange city, especially in a strange country where you can't even see the street signs. In the rear of some of the buses there are only a few seats in order to allow for more standing room, so people are used to standing.

The weather was cool that day, but inside the bus it was hot and stuffy from all the body heat. People were crammed in, bodies up against one another, like so many sardines in a can. I was clutching my briefcase and umbrella with one hand, holding onto the back of a seat with the other.

Despite heavy traffic, Italian buses move rapidly once they get going. You must hold on tight or else you'll fall. Unless, of course, the bus is packed, in which case you couldn't fall over if you tried. In fact, sometimes your behind is right up against another's, which can be kind of nice, depending on whose butt is doing the rubbing!

Buses in Italy are a neat place from which to see the sights, practice reading signs in Italian, and watch people. I like the official notice posted inside the bus that instructs passengers to give their seats "to women, the elderly, and the disabled." I think that's a nice reflection of the culture.

People don't smile much while riding the buses, or in public for that matter. They pretty much pretend to be minding their own business. But you wonder what they are thinking. Do they know I am not one of them? Can they tell I am a *straniero*? An *Americano*? Is someone sizing me up, looking at me as just another pocket to be picked?

The man standing behind me was facing forward, his hand hanging at his side. He was looking straight ahead but I had the uneasy feeling that his hand, if it had eyes, was scoping out my pockets. He was nicely dressed, almost dapper, and was sporting a three- to four-day-old growth of facial hair like most Italian men. Before I could figure out what was happening, I felt something brush against my body. Then, inside my pocket, something moved. It was so weird! It was just like I had read about. It was his hand! I looked at him and he looked at me. He didn't smile, and neither did I. "Signor," I said, "what is your hand doing in my pocket?"

At that moment, I rolled over, opened my eyes, and realized that I must have been dreaming! Or was I? I guess I had heard so much about the pickpockets and the gypsies that I'd become psychotic about it.

Maybe I was just lucky, or maybe it was the Saint Christopher medal Gloria gave me before I left that was protecting me. At any rate, I can honestly say that I never had anything stolen or taken from me, and I don't recall having lost anything of value during the whole trip, though there were some close calls. So, why was I so paranoid?

All the sources of information were saying the same thing. People I talked to, books and bulletins I read, all gave the same warning: BE CAREFUL! Like this tourist advisory written for business travelers to Italy:

> *Buy a money belt before going to Italy. Don't flash money in public places. And, watch out for the zingari (the gypsies)!*
>
> *Sophia Loren once played a thief who was working the buses. With razor blade concealed in her mouth, she would cut the straps of handbags.*
>
> *The Termini Railway Station in Rome is notorious. Among high-risk bus routes: the 64 to Saint Peter's and the 46, 81, and 492, all serving tourist areas, of course. You are advised to avoid the Piazza Navone and Villa Borghese areas after dark.*
>
> *American Express and Visa have special programs to protect cardholders from loss due to accident or theft while renting cars abroad. But Italy is often excepted, due to its high rate of theft.*

What is going on here? Are Italians all crooks? Do you really have to watch your back at all times? Are conditions of personal safety any worse in Italy than in the United States? I mean, you shouldn't go walking in Central Park after dark, either, right?

. . .

While immersing myself in Italian culture and Italian language in preparation for the trip, Gloria and I had managed to find a copy of "*Il Ladro di Bicicletta*" ("*The Bicycle Thief*"), a classic Italian movie that portrays conditions in Italy after World War II. It is a heart-rending story showing not only the destitution and hard times of that era, but the determination to overcome so many adverse conditions.

The hero's wife sells the bed linens and other essential household stuff to get money to buy a bicycle, which the husband (*il marito*) needs to get a job hanging posters around town. While he is up on a ladder working, someone steals the bicycle, his only means of transportation and livelihood. Much of the rest of the movie involves the hero's escapades in chasing the thief. The moral of the story is that Italians themselves are often victims of pickpockets and petty crimes.

The incidence of these petty crimes is not evenly distributed by city or region. The crime rate is much higher in the South, in Naples, for example, than elsewhere, especially if you ask someone from the North. Unemployment (around 20%) is significantly higher in the South, too.

Now, it pains me to have to say this because, after all, my father's family came from the Naples area (region of Campagnia) and my mother's family came from even further south, the island of Sicily. I began thinking that maybe all the good people, like my grandpas, are the ones who left. Maybe the people who stayed had no choice but to become crooks because they were starving. Or maybe they were already doing so well as crooks in the first place that there was no incentive for them to leave. Who knows?! (For the other side of the story, an excellent historical portrayal of how Italian immigrants to America were ripped off and taken unfair advantage of, see *La Storia: Five Centuries of the Italian American Experience,* Jerre Mangione & Ben Morreale, New York: HarperCollins Publishers, 1992.)

On the serious side, I do know that during my entire stay in Italy, I never actually saw a pickpocket nor did I meet anyone (with one exception) who led me to believe that he or she was probably a crook.

But, when you see all the security precautions over there, something I refer to as the "Fortress Mentality," you have to believe that there must be security problems. Double and triple locks abound on the doors and windows. Gates, walls, fences, and shutters are conspicuously prevalent and surround the houses, shops and stores. Dogs are commonly used for protection. You have to believe that there must be at least the potential for a fair amount of criminal activity.

For example, consider the *Antoniolli* brand of door lock, which is used widely throughout Italy. I had heard it described before the trip but words cannot do it justice. When you see one in operation, it is fascinating! Gloria and I videotaped a demonstration of the one in the apartment.

The locking system consists of steel rods worked by ratchets. The rods go up into the framework above the door and into the flooring below. You have a great big old-fashioned key that has to be cranked around four times to lock (or to unlock) the door. With each successive crank of 360 degrees, the rods move further into the floor and up into the wood framework. By the time you've gone around four times, that baby is locked up like a steel vault! In fact, the appearance from the inside resembles a bank vault. In addition, many doors have a separate deadbolt lock, which uses a smaller key and needs to be cranked only twice. (This is what my apartment had.)

Business establishments in Italy are also very security conscious. For example, the people at the neighborhood dry cleaners that I patronized were friendly enough. But their door was always locked, even when they were open for business! To get in, you had to press a buzzer and then someone inside hits a remote switch to let you in. Inside, a large dog camps out next to the counter, watching your every move.

As you might expect, banks have the ultimate in controlled access. The one I saw made use of an elaborate double-entry system. Now I was aware that Italians invented double-entry bookkeeping, but did not realize the extent to which they've applied the concept of double entry to customer access.

My neighborhood bank had a double entry door. You pressed a buzzer to release the first door; then, after being permitted to enter the small glass enclosed vestibule, you waited for the first door to shut behind you before pressing another buzzer for the second door (in front of you) to open. You are like a rat in a trap, and in full view of everyone inside and outside the place including the uniformed guard who is in close proximity and within full view.

Maybe now you can see why I refer to this phenomenon as a Fortress Mentality. And there is a very logical rationale for it, in my mind, at least. If one considers the geographic exposure of the Italian peninsula, its magnificent coastline has been a real magnet over the centuries for invasion. There was always someone coming and going. If it wasn't Napoleon, then it was Ferdinand II, or Charlemagne, or the Greeks, or the Bourbons, or the Spanish.

There is a psychological and attitudinal aspect of Fortress Mentality as well as the physical. Italian people will not become best friends with you overnight. It takes time. Italians are known to have a guarded facial expression as if they don't want anyone to know what they are thinking, because to do so could display a weakness in the persona.

So, in my view, Fortress Mentality is an instinctive pattern of behavior by a people who have always had to be concerned about their safety and well-being, regardless of who was supposedly in charge at the time. As my Greek friend, Nick, so aptly put it, "After centuries of oppression, the Italians are naturally suspicious of government."

When you consider Italian taxes and the heavy hand of government in people's everyday lives, Italians must feel like someone always has hands in their pockets. There is a tax for everything, with a big value-added tax (15–20% in many cases) on top of that. There is a TV tax for the privilege of owning and operating a television set in your own home! There is a fee for packages left at the post office that are undeliverable, a kind of storage fee. Someone once said that if Italians actually paid all of their taxes, it would amount to 150 percent!

. . .

When talking with Italians, it's best to avoid three subjects: politics, religion, and crime. If, however, you ignore the prohibition against talking about crime, you'll find that someone always makes the point about the low incidence of *violent* crime (murders, shootings, etc.), especially compared with the USA. "What's wrong with America?" they ask. I was told time and time again that in Italia thieves might steal your stuff or pick your pockets clean, but at least they are not going to kill you.

I followed up on this and did some library research on crime statistics for Italy versus other countries but it is difficult to draw conclusions when the definitions for the various data sets are not strictly comparable.

The Country Commercial Guide for Italy published by the U.S. Embassy in Rome, for example, says that Italy has a very low rate of violent crime, little of which is directed toward tourists. Petty crime (pick pocketing, theft from parked cars, purse snatching) is a significant problem, especially in large cities. Most thefts occur at crowded tourist sites, on public buses, or at the major railway stations, including Rome's Termini, Milan's Centrale,

Florence's Santa Maria Novella, and the Centrale in Naples.

In retrospect, I would have to say that the number of criminals in Italy is probably no greater than in the USA, on a per capita basis. Based on my own limited experience, in fact, I would say that Italian cities are safer than ours. In Rome, Torino, Venice, Florence, and Milan, I never felt seriously threatened or really scared. And I did not always stay strictly within the main tourist areas, or on busy commercial streets.

. . .

Although I, personally, was not a victim of crime in Italy, I did know some—mainly among the students—who were, or seemed to be. Even in those instances, however, it was often a case of stuff lost or misplaced rather than stolen. For example,

> Ken lost his watch when some guy pulled it off of his wrist at a disco down by the river in the wee hours of the morning.
> James lost and then recovered a shirt at a hotel in Santa Marguerita.
> Jenn lost her camera.
> Professor Bob, who went to Torino to teach the year after I did, had his pocket picked and therefore "lost" his billfold.
> Nicole got top honors for losing the most stuff, which she refers to in the yearbook under the heading "Times When I Was Most Bent." She says "lost my camera in Cinque Terra, my rings in Rapallo, my daypack in Aosta, and my VISA in a machine in Torre Pellice." Priceless!

Now, this is not to say that I was totally free of adverse incidents myself. There were several things that happened to me that could be classified as close calls: (1) a potential theft of our baggage due to a run-in with a shady character in Naples, (2) an actual break-in of our luggage at the train station in Milan, (3) a battle with an Italian ATM that *took* my money, (4) an experience with an Italian casino that did the same, and (5) an encounter with two young female gypsies in front of the *duomo* (cathedral) in Milan.

. . .

Yes, we did have a threatening experience in Naples, even though we did not spend any significant amount of time there. It was in the Naples train station as Gloria and I were passing through on our way from Rome to Sorrento. This character introduces himself as a porter. He was in his mid- or late 30s, a stocky, robust man of medium height with a very assertive demeanor.

I didn't really believe he was a porter because I had never seen one at any of the train stations before and, besides, all the tour books warn that you should be prepared to carry your own stuff when going by train because Italian train stations do not have porters. But this guy pretended to be one anyway, and I guess I went along with him partly out of curiosity and partly from a desire to help the less fortunate people of the South where jobs are scarce. Maybe, just maybe, the guy was trying to earn an honest buck.

He approached and asked if we needed a cab. When I told him "No, we were going to catch the train for Sorrento," he said he would show us where to find it. Well, I already knew that you have to go downstairs below the main terminal to catch the little commuter train called the *Circumvesuviana* that serves Sorrento, Vesuvius, and Pompeii because I had been there before. I should have just told him to go away at that point, but I was leery of what he might do if provoked. So, we went along with his offer to help and just followed him, as though he were doing us a favor.

The man kept insisting on carrying one of our bags but every time he did, I refused. At one point, we almost had a tug-of-war. I was certain the guy had no official capacity but didn't want to upset him either, because I could see that he was part of a larger operation. As we moved through the terminal, it became apparent that he had friends all around, including the guy who was selling the tickets for the little train. Not knowing what he and his friends might do, not seeing any police around, and especially because Gloria was with me, I wanted to avoid a confrontation.

Upon buying the tickets, I turned to the man, gave him a 10,000 lire tip (about $6.50) for his trouble and told him *Buon Natale* (Merry Christmas). He acted like that wasn't enough so I gave him another 10,000 lire and walked away. And that was that.

I know now it was probably stupid of me to keep following him like I did. He was walking at a brisk pace and at one point even led us outside the main terminal, taking a shortcut to the lower level. At that point he could easily have led us into a trap and run off with our stuff.

You would think that an unpleasant experience like this would dispel the affinity I have for train stations. On the contrary, I think they are a neat place to hang out because they bustle. People and trains coming and going. Colorful announcements booming over the P.A., as when the baritone voice is announcing the train and track numbers, in Italian, of course, of arrivals and departures. My favorite is the number 555. It just sounds so cool: *Cinque Cento Cinquanta Cinque (*pronounced CHEEN'-KWAY CHAYN'-TOW CHEEN-KWAN'-TA CHEEN'-KWAY).

The atmosphere of an Italian train station is like that of a bazaar. Snack bars, shops, and newsstands invite you to partake of their goodies, like some big open market with a roof on top. You can buy English language newspapers there, like the *International Herald Tribune* and *USA Today*. You can enjoy a *cappuccino, espresso, briosche, pizza,* or *dolce* while waiting for your train to arrive. There are also information and tourist offices, sometimes helpful, sometimes not, along with baggage check and other services. And, of course, the indispensable public *toilette,* sometimes called W.C., pronounced VEE' CHEE.

Throughout the trip, I had ample opportunity to explore not only train stations in Italy but also ones in Switzerland, Germany, and Austria. One of the differences is the operation of the baggage check. In Italy, it tends to be a manual operation, meaning there is a large room full of luggage tended by two or more persons who serve the customer from behind a counter. This is in contrast to some of the other countries where there is more reliance on coin operated, self-serve lockers of varying sizes to perform the same function. In Munich, for example, I was able to leave my luggage in a self-service locker upon arrival so I could walk around town looking for a hotel unencumbered.

. . .

Toward the very end of the trip, Gloria and I had an unexpected experience with the baggage check in Milan. After departing Torino for the last time and embarking on a 10-day tour prior to the flight home, we checked our two biggest and heaviest pieces of luggage at the Milan train station so we could retrieve them on the way back immediately prior to our flight. I debated whether to tell the baggage check people we were leaving our stuff for 10 days, because I thought that might be an invitation for pilferage. Mark also thought it was best not to tell them. So we didn't.

When we returned to Milan to claim our baggage, we did not notice anything unusual. Mark was with us at the time as he had met us earlier in the day to show us the sights of Milan—the Galleria, the Duomo, and La Scala—and he helped us claim the luggage and carry it to the airport bus before bidding us *arrivederci.* We needed to get to a hotel near the airport where we had reservations for our final overnight stay in Italy.

Well, after the bus dropped us off at the airport, while waiting for a taxi to take us to the hotel, I happened to notice that the lock on my suitcase had been tampered with. In fact, it was *rotto* (broken)! What an eerie feeling. I couldn't believe my eyes! I examined it more closely. Yep, it was *rotto,* alright!

My first thought was that somebody must have stolen the borrowed laptop computer inside and, of course, I would have to pay to replace it. To my amazement, they had not! Gloria's suitcase had been tampered with, too, but apparently not broken into.

When we arrived at our hotel, we went through everything to see what else might have been missing. Nothing, or so it appeared. Then, Gloria observed that maybe they did not take anything out but rather put something in! Now that was a scary thought!

So, at that point, we took everything out of both pieces of our luggage and inspected every inch of the suitcases themselves: the lining, the pockets, the handles, the zippers, the wheels, everything. This was the last thing we wanted to do at this late hour. We were tired, the stuff in our suitcases, including many gift items, had been carefully packed very snugly, and we would have to repack it all! What a mess! What a day.

To this day, we do not know what the true story was behind this incident. Could it be that someone in the baggage check was on the verge of breaking open the luggage but got interrupted? Or, as Mark later suggested, could it have been the police? About a month after we returned home, Mark sent me a fax to apologize for giving me "the wrong advice concerning your luggage that you left at the train station in Milan." He went on to explain:

> *I remember I told you not to say anything to them about how long you were going to leave your luggage there. After speaking with Jera about someone going into your suitcase, she thinks that maybe the police opened your suitcase to see if someone left a bomb there. They probably became concerned because no one came to claim it for many days (you were gone over a week), and the luggage attendants got worried. Anyway, as long as nothing was stolen I guess it is okay.*

• • •

Surely the funniest thing that happened to me in Italy was a pseudo pick pocketing event that took place right there in the hallowed halls of the *Scuola*, i.e., the school. It was in the form of the ATM machine gone berserk.

> *On Friday, the ATM ate my money! It said, "Take your money and card" but when I went to grab the 300,000 Lire (that's about $200), it sucked it right back into the machine, right through my fingers!! Jera called the bank and argued with them in Italian for me (they wanted me to go back to my home bank to get the money). Now, I have to wait 'til Thursday when they balance the machine. This is Italy and nothing is easy here!*

I had to wait a couple of weeks before Jera got a phone call instructing me to stop by one of the branch locations to pick up my money. I had to show my passport and argue with the manager first, which I believe is standard procedure. Then I got my money! That's the way it works in Italy.

• • •

Yet another opportunity for someone to take my money occurred at a casino in St. Vincent, a town in the mountains of the bilingual region of *Valle d' Aosta,* north of Torino. The mountain scenery on the ride up there was magnificent.

I took the money I got back from the ATM to the casino to see if I could double or triple it, but the slots had other ideas. Besides having to pay 20,000 lire (about $14) just to get inside, I would soon discover that the machines were in a very stubborn mood. No fun at all!

> *Since there was a train strike, I took the bus to St. Vincent on Friday and returned on Saturday night. There is a casino there but the slots only want to take your money and not return any so I didn't spend much time there. St. Vincent is nestled in the Alpine mountains an hour and a half north of Torino, near France. It's a pretty little village with cute shops, an old church, and a funicular (sp?) that takes you up the mountain to the mineral baths where people go for their health. The scenery is fantastic. They're big on Grappa (liquor), and woodcarvings. All the street signs are in both Italian and French.*

. . .

After three-and-one-half months in Italy, I thought it was amazing that we had yet to encounter a single gypsy, much less a band of gypsies (*zingari* in Italian, one of those fascinating Italian words you quickly fall in love with). Yes, there was a woman I saw begging for money in Rome. She was lying on the stoop in front of St. John Lateran Church holding a baby. She and the child looked unclean and poor. She might have been a gypsy, I don't know. I didn't ask her.

There are stories about the *zingari* stealing from your car, or taking money out of your pockets. There are stories about how they will distract you, such as a group of gypsy children running up and surrounding you, yelling, shoving and begging for money, while at the same time one of them has a hand inside your pocket. There are other stories of gypsies shoving newspapers in your face to distract you or tossing a live baby at you so you have to catch it. Then, they grab your things while you are busy with the newspapers or the baby.

Well, the day before our departure from Italy when Mark met us in Milan, as we stood in front of the cathedral on the *Piazza Del Duomo* we were approached by two young gypsies. Right in front of that marvelous Duomo with its 2,245 full size statues (!) nestled among the spires. There among the hundreds of other people standing around, talking, looking, taking pictures. In the middle of this huge rectangular *piazza* that is the social center of the city. Two young women walked up to us and began speaking Italian. And how did I know they were gypsies? Hah! I knew it even before they said anything. Because one of them was carrying newspapers and the other a baby!

As soon as they approached, I looked at them and shouted *"No! Va! Va!"* Well, if looks could kill, one of them was giving me the evil eye. Mark reacted more slowly and I couldn't tell whether he was aware of what was happening or not. I was holding tightly onto our mini camcorder concealed under my jacket and keeping my distance. I told them to go (*"Va! Va!"*) and they did. And that was the end of our sole encounter with *zingari*.

11

CONNECTION

A man who has not been in Italy is always conscious of an inferiority.
—Dr. Samuel Johnson (1709–1784) English author and lexicographer

What a wonderful feeling to realize that you are in some way connected to so many others. Not just family and friends, mind you, but others with whom you share experiences, thoughts, and values. Others you have known but will never see again. Others you have never met but whose words you have read, or heard about. Others to whom you are bound only by the affection of mutual understanding and common ideals.

• • •

October is Italian-American Heritage Month, a time for celebrating the contributions of 26 million Americans of Italian descent—fifth-largest ethnic group in the United

States of America. Popular sports and entertainment figures like Frank Sinatra, Dean Martin, Perry Como, Tony Bennett, Joe Dimaggio, Yogi Berra, Rocky Marciano, and Tony Danza. And a few surprises—namely, Edward DeBartolo, Mr. Peanut, Harry Warren, Mother Frances Cabrini, Rosie the Riveter, Susan Sarandon, Bruce Springsteen, Wynona Judd, and Regis Filbin.

October is also a time for celebrating the contributions to America of other famous Italians, like Christopher Columbus, Amerigo Vespucci, Garibaldi, the Cabots of Boston, the Great Caruso, and Rudolph Valentino. When I was a boy, we always celebrated Columbus Day on October 12, because that was the day in 1492 when Chris and his crew first sighted land. We knew who Columbus was and why he was important. We knew the names of the three famous ships which sailed under his command, and that he had to rely on the support of the Queen of Spain for his voyage because, in 1492, there was no Italy!

It is easy to feel a sense of pride and affinity with Italy, especially when you consider the many artistic, political, and scientific contributions to America and the world that have come from the country shaped like a boot. Italy has given us the poetry of Dante, the art of Michelangelo and other artists of the Renaissance, the science of Galileo, the music of Verdi and Puccini.

In addition to the many great explorers and composers, Italian filmmakers have become famous the world over and so have her designers, car manufacturers, footballers, bicyclists, and race car drivers. For better or for worse, Italy produced the first international banking system and many other financial and accounting innovations. Italian architects influenced and embellished the design of the Capitol in Washington, D.C.

. . .

The notion of "connection" begins to take on new meaning when you think about the flow of people and ideas, back and forth, across the oceans over many years. Italians and Italian-Americans alike. From Italy to America, and back again. If Italy is, to a degree, a reflection of some American values, it is due in no small part to the accomplishments and influence of the millions of Italians who emigrated to America, then sent money and ideas back to Italy in return. But the real catalyst for American orientation in Italy has been political and economic.

Italy is one of the largest democracies in Europe. The major ruling political party (the Christian-Democratic party, or CD) for many years, was committed to a "Western" concept of individualism and capitalism, despite the fascist history and strong post-War communist influence. The CD thrived as an "American" party, not only in the sense that it has been pro-American, but that it steered the evolution of Italy into a materialistic and consumer society.

In terms of standard of living, the Italian economy has, by and large, caught up with the rest of Europe. The "necessities," such as remote-control color television, dishwashers, freezers, push-button phones, etc., are as available in Italy as in most Western countries. Not so with microwaves or clothes dryers, but that is another story.

Other signs of Americanization and Westernization are, perhaps, less admirable: fewer people going to church, more people using contraceptives and living together outside of marriage. Italians now can get a divorce, have abortions, and purchase pornographic material, unlike in years past. It is the development of a lifestyle that, for the most part, incorporates an adaptation of the many positive and negative aspects of the "American way of life."

• • •

One of the fringe benefits of the trip was that much of what I learned abroad would be valuable information to share with my students back home: details about the products, the stores, the advertising, and other cross-cultural phenomena that relate directly or indirectly to marketing, retailing, product management, or entrepreneurship.

In today's world, it's become extremely important to give our future business leaders education and training about other countries. Hence, aspects of business and marketing that are characterized as *global*, *cross-cultural*, and *international* are now valued more highly than ever before. Accordingly, I began to capitalize on this opportunity by incorporating into my classes much of what I had learned during my stay in Italy. The students were immediately receptive.

Another stroke of luck was that, within months after my return, I was asked to teach a Special Topics course about the trip! The title we gave it was "Cross Cultural Consumer Behavior: An Italian Perspective." The students referred to it as "The Italy Class."

In this class, I tried to give students a feel for what it would be like to actually go to Italy (or any other foreign country) to do business there. But "Doing Business in Italy" was only a small part of the course.

Students were required to immerse themselves in the culture and history of Italy, learn a bit of the language, familiarize themselves with the geography as well as the customs, traditions, and etiquette and, best of all, with Italian music and Italian food! It was fun for all of us. At the heart of the course was my belief that in order to know how to do business in a foreign country—any country—one must first learn all those other things about the region and the people, so that they will see that you care enough to do your homework. You care enough to learn something about them. It is a matter of honor and respect. And it's just good common sense, isn't it? "When in Rome, you do as the Romans do."

The Europeans, by the way, are much better at this than we. Many Europeans speak three, four, or five languages—and speak them fluently. They must, I suppose, since the distances between the countries are like the distances between our states. So we Americans have a lot of catching up to do if we are going to compete successfully in the global marketplace.

The students in The Italy Class also had to do a socially oriented project. I told them to choose a subject like the music, the food, or an Italian wedding. Well, none of them were very musically inclined, and no one was planning to get married in the near future, so they all chose to do something related to the food. Surprise!

Many signed up for the weekly food project, taking turns preparing and bringing various Italian dishes to class. We had bruschetta. We had Amaretto cheesecake and Italian pasta salad. We had espresso and biscotti. Once we got this thing rolling, we ate well every week, and that's how we would begin class—by eating. Someone even joked about everyone lining up for their food, not at all in the manner of true Italians!

And of course we had pizza, courtesy of a small group of students who chose to make homemade pizza for their project. On a Sunday evening they met at the home of Jim and Janice Kremer who were planning a first trip to Italy that year, and who have since become good friends. The group made pizza from scratch and videotaped the whole event for the rest of the class. Gloria and I were invited to observe and to eat. They did a great job.

Another group, actually most of the class, decided to put on a dinner at an Italian restaurant. It was set up buffet style so that we could sample different entrees, and wine-tasting was included, too. Gloria and I were there to observe and to eat, of course. I later discuss this with Mark in an e-mail, continuing to have fun with the minestrone thing:

> Hey Mark,
>
> Have a nice weekend! Tonight the students from my Italy class are putting on a special dinner with a wine-tasting at an Italian restaurant. And my friend, Bruno, the Italian language instructor will be there, too. I'll think of you as we enjoy all that good ITALIAN-AMERICAN food, Mark!
> —Peter
> P.S. Yes, they have minestrone, too.

Mark responded in kind:

> Peter,
> Buon apettito! But it ain't an Italian restaurant if they serve minestrone soup. You know they don't have minestrone in Italy!
> Mark

. . .

I was still keeping in touch with Giuseppina and at about this time decided to e-mail her about my latest exploits. And to try out my Italian once again. For those of you whose Italian may be a little rusty, let me explain in general what the following communiqué is all about. Then, before I give you the exact translation, try to read it on your own and see how much of it you can make out. EVEN IF YOU DON'T KNOW ANY ITALIAN AT ALL, TRY IT. You'll be surprised at how recognizable some of the words may be!

In general, I was telling Giuseppina of my continuing efforts to maintain a connection with Italian culture. Also, since I was feeling pretty confident about my ability to compose a letter in Italian, I decided to stick my neck out (at the end of the message) and ask for a critique.

Now, see if you can follow some of the thoughts being expressed (remember that *per favore* means "please," and *grazie* means "thank you.").

> Cara Giuseppina,
> Ricorda mi? Sono Pietro Carusone, il professore visitando dagli Stati Uniti.
> Come sta Lei, bene? Come sta la suo marito? Mi molgie e io abbiamo visitato la bella citta di New Orleans due settimane fa. Conosce New Orleans? La' abbiamo vista un bel piazza si chiama Piazza d'Italia! Anche, era una parata grande dalla societa d'Italiano-Americani! Sa Lei chi era il presidente honorario di questa parata? Sonny Bono! Hah!!
> Io e miei quattro filii abbiamo unito la societa qui in Dayton, Ohio si chiama Filii d'Italia d'America. Questa primavera e estate saremo giocare bocce ball! Piaciamo bocce ball, e Lei?
> Per favore, mi dica se ce sono multi sbagli in questa e-mail.
> Grazie e tanto auguri!
> Buon Pasqua.
> Peter

All right, if you understood every word of my Easter greeting to Giuseppina, then you can skip the next part. Otherwise, here is the translation, paragraph by paragraph:

1. After the salutation ("Dear Giuseppina,"), I say "Remember me?" and then reintroduce myself as the "visiting professor" from the United States.

2. I am asking how she and her husband are doing. I tell her about a trip with my wife to New Orleans two weeks earlier, and our discovery of the "Piazza d'Italia" (Italy Square) there, and about the big Italian-American parade we saw with Sonny Bono as honorary Marshall. I presume she has heard of Sonny Bono.
3. I share with her the fact that my four sons and I joined the Sons of Italy Lodge in Dayton and are looking forward to competing in the bocce ball league in spring and summer.
4. In the very short fourth paragraph, I ask her to "please tell me if there are many mistakes in this e-mail."
5. The close simply says thanks, good wishes, and Happy Easter!

Giuseppina's response was, as always, polite and cordial. As you will see, she would intersperse paragraphs of English with paragraphs of Italian, something I often did in my e-mails to Italians. In this particular case, to comply with my request for a critique, she actually rewrites my whole letter, inserts it in the middle of her e-mail, and sends it back to me:

Caro Pietro,

I am receiving the E-mail properly again. I am verry sorry but something was wrong with the connection and so I lose your greetings for Easter and many other I suppose. Please excusme.

Well, I have to tell you that the letter you wrote in italiano contein some mistakes. Now I will sent it back to you in a correct manner:

Cara Giuseppina, mi ricorda? Sono Pietro Carusone, il professore in visita dagli Stati Uniti.

Lei come sta, bene? Come sta la sua famiglia in Alba? Mia moglie ed io abbiamo visitato la bella citta di New Orleans due settimane fa. Conosce New Orleans? Abbiamo visto una bella piazza che si chiama Piazza d'Italia! C'era anche una grande parata della societa di Italo-Americani. Lei sa chi era il Presidente onorario di questa parata? Sonny Bono! Hah!!

Io e i miei quattro figli abbiamo unito la societa qui in Dayton, si chiama Figli d'Italia d'America. Questa primavera ed estate giocheremo a bocce. A noi piacciono le bocce, e a lei?

Per favore mi dica se ci sono molti sbagli in questa e-mail.

Grazie e tanti auguri.

Come vedi non c'erano troppi sbagli, solo qualcuno....chissa quanti errori faccio io in inglese!! Io non ho mai visitato New Orleans, per mi piace giocare a bocce.

Tanti cari auguri anche a te
La tua amica
Giuseppina

She says that my letter contains "some" mistakes. Haha! Well, if you compare the two versions, word-by-word, about 50 percent of the words in my letter were wrong, far more than the few errors in her English to me! I guess that's not bad. I mean, actually, 500 is a great batting average, isn't it?!

Of course, Giuseppina was still being ever gracious and generous with her appraisal of my language skills. In case you didn't catch it, in her final paragraph she says "As you can see, there are not too many mistakes, only a few...who knows how many errors I make in English!!"

It is a wonderful feeling to realize that you are in some way connected with others who have experienced the same thing as you, or who are about to. More so when they are people who happen to be thousands of miles away in a foreign land. I guess that's why I have welcomed the chance to keep in touch with people like Giuseppina. And Mark. And Jera.

And, on this side of the Atlantic, there are people like Caroline and Terry, and Bruno, who helped Gloria and me to prepare for our trip. Also, Bob and Loraine, Ben and Barbara, whom we, in turn, were able to advise when they were making plans for their respective journeys abroad. It kind of confirms that we really are all connected.

When I think of those who have helped created these connections for me, my family is at the top of the list. Especially my grandpa, my dad, my mother, aunts and uncles, and others who taught me from an early age about the rich heritage and responsibility that comes with being Italian. The sense of pride and joy in celebrating life. The strong work ethic. The love of food, music, and people.

A former colleague, Jane, believed in the notion that "passing it on" was a way of life—and she and her husband lived it. Whenever given the opportunity to help younger people learn and pull themselves up, she saw it as a chance to pay back, so to speak, the people who had helped *her* when she was first starting out. What goes around comes around.

Now, this may sound strange, but the web of people with whom I feel connected with regard to Italy goes beyond the family and friends mentioned above. There are others, those who are known to me only by their written words. Like author Tim Parks and the lovable characters who inhabit his *Italian Neighborhood*. And Frances Mayes, *Tuscan Sun* authoress, whose adventures during academic holiday are easy for me to identify with, and to envy! Then, there's Mario Puzo, Luigi Barzini, Jerre Mangione, and Ben Morreale, whose vivid descriptions and depictions of Italian life have left their mark on my mind and in my heart. And others who have gone before and have passed on their thoughts and ideas to me, and to generation after generation.

Back in the 1960s, I read the book *From Dream to Discovery: On Being a Scientist* by Hans Selye. It made a big impression on me and I copied several passages that I have kept with me all these years. One of these comes to mind now because it suggests that one does not have to be related by blood in order to be connected.

> *"...for who is my brother? The man of my blood, even if we have nothing else in common— or the man of my mind, to whom I am bound only by the warmth of mutual understanding and common ideals?"*

There is and has been for centuries a virtual cavalcade of people visiting Italy, a steady stream of humanity who for one reason or another have entered that magical world, only to absorb bits and pieces and return home transformed. On a rather grand scale, there has been the inevitable procession of those in the community of Italians, Italian-Americans, and wannabes alike, exchanging, contributing, and integrating the cultures.

There are those who would help each other make the journey by mapping out the delights and the pitfalls. Just as I was helped by others who had gone before, and now am in a position to help others who plan themselves to make the journey.

We are all part of a larger community, one that spans the centuries and continents, bonded together by our love of Italy. We are truly connected.

・ ・ ・

POSTSCRIPT: As I rewrite this chapter, Mark is only weeks away from moving back to the States, to San Diego. It is interesting to note that after all these months of writing to me in English, all of a sudden he now is writing his e-mails in Italian! I told him, Mark, you say you can't wait to leave, but now you are writing in Italian because you miss Italy already! So far he has ignored my comment.

12

DON TOUCHA DA BANANA!

The compass was discovered by Flavio Gioia of Amalfi in 1302. The condom was invented by Gabriele Falloppio, native of Modena, in the 16th century. And the ice cream cone was created by Italo Marcioni, an Italian immigrant to New Jersey, USA.

Despite many similarities between the consumer marketplace of Italy and that of the United States, it is the differences that are fascinating. The food, the shopping, and the array of unique products are, in my opinion, among the most intriguing features of the Italian landscape. The Italians are a highly creative and innovative people. Hundreds of great inventions can be traced to the genius, vision and practical spirit of the Italians.

The main focus of this chapter is on the Italian consumer society, while product innovation is a closely related subtopic. What is it like living and shopping in Italy, from a consumer perspective? How are consumers treated and what kind of service can one expect? Are there certain things to watch for, certain taboo behaviors to avoid, so that people don't think you are an idiot, or a *stupido americano*?!

The first part of this chapter highlights a few of the many unique products I observed in Italy, including some bedroom and bathroom oddities, the garbage dumpsters that they keep in the street at curbside because there is no place else to put them, and the tiny little vehicles called APES (pronounced AH' PAYS) that run all over the city making deliveries.

The second part of the chapter will give practical suggestions for everyday shopping. Here is where I present my list of Useful Tips and Consumer-Friendly Advice for Hassle Free Shopping in Italy. Did you know, for example, that you are not supposed to touch the bananas?

· · ·

As a professor of marketing, I was naturally interested in examining the products of Italy and its consumer shopping patterns, especially with my background in retailing and marketing research, and because one of the courses I regularly teach is about new products. Likewise, I was interested in how people shop, the kind of service they receive, store locations, hours of operation, and so on.

So, I took notes, made lists, and even asked my students in the *Scuola* to do the same. We looked everywhere for new products—in the shops and restaurants, in public restrooms, in people's homes, and while walking along the street.

Now, some of the products that caught my eye were more conspicuous than others—the shutters, for example. Imagine *you* are walking down the street and happen to notice that all the windows, even on balconies, have shutters. These are pull-down contraptions that almost look like garage doors. When they're closed, they not only keep out light, but can be padlocked and secured from outside entry. If you happen to be walking by when the stores are closed, you might not even know that there are stores there. All you would see is a deserted street with buildings bolted up, the fronts of which look almost like warehouse buildings.

Another product that caught my eye was the garbage dumpster. When I moved into the apartment in Torino, I had asked where to put the garbage. Well, the answer was "in the street!" At least, that's what I thought I heard. Actually, it was "in the dumpster in the street!"

It's true—right in front of almost every building in the street at curbside are one or more mini-dumpsters, about the size of an American made SUV. No need to use garbage cans; just take your plastic bags of trash directly to the dumpster. A drawback, of course, is that for every dumpster sitting at curbside, there is that much less parking space.

Space in general is at a premium in Italy. Population density, of course, is very high. Also, the natural resources and raw materials that we in the States take for granted are mostly lacking. Italy has no oil, no iron, no coal. Vast areas of the land are difficult to cultivate. Most of the primary products needed for economic growth have to be imported. This impacts products, lifestyles, and consumption habits.

As in other European countries, the cost of gasoline in Italy is several times what Americans have been used to. And with few residential garages or driveways (parking cars on the sidewalk is a common practice), it is no wonder that almost everyone seems to drive a tiny little Fiat *macchina* (automobile) or *Vespa* scooter!

Lack of space and natural resources accounts for the kind of vehicles you see on the streets, the extent to which people utilize public transportation, and the popularity of neighborhood stores for daily shopping. It is common to see little cars like the *Cinque Cento* (Fiat 500) and Italian sports cars, but virtually no American cars and very few Japanese imports.

Which brings us to the *APE*. The APE is a unique small delivery vehicle used to move large quantities of stuff around town. Their cargo is often piled high above the cab. When it is running, the APE sounds like it is powered by a lawn mower engine! I was curious about the name, and several times wrote to Mark to inquire. First I got a lot of teasing: "It means monkey," he wrote. "Get a clue!" Then he passed on words from a colleague: ". . . very dangerous . . . the easiest way to die." I persisted. Finally I got the true meaning:

"APE means bee. We just looked it up in the dictionary. It is not an abbreviation or acronym. Max says it stands for 'When you turn the wheel, you fly like a bee.' So there you go."

. . .

A word of caution about the authenticity of the products that I believed to be "unique." In fact, some of them may not be totally unique to Italy. They might be available in other countries, including the USA. I just don't know. It is quite possible that some of the products that tickled my fancy may be typical of Europe, in general, and not just Italy.

For example, here are several "unique" products I spotted in the display windows of Italian stores:

- A baby spoon with the handle at a 45-degree angle. Makes feeding baby easier, not as awkward as with a straight-handled spoon.
- A toddler's jigsaw puzzle made with large pieces with a knob on each piece, easier for children to grasp. Great idea!
- Collars and matching cuffs on a mannequin in the display window of a women's wear shop. Very

stylish! We have them here, I am told, though I have never seen them.
- A cute little disposable toothbrush with a glob of toothpaste already on it that I bought from a vending machine in a restaurant men's room. Designed for one-time use, the mini-toothbrush is packaged inside a small plastic tube and costs less than a dollar. It is a tiny little brush, made in Italy. I brought one home to share with my students. A great product concept and one of my favorites!

Another interesting product innovation caught my attention at one of the train stations. It was a feature I observed on the luggage carts, an automatic lock to brake the wheels, similar to the shut-off safety feature on power lawn mowers in the USA. Squeeze the handle and it releases the brake. Carts can't roll when not in use. What a great idea. Why don't they apply this to supermarket carts?

. . .

The students had their favorite products, too. When I asked them to make a list of unique product ideas they had seen in Italy, everyone had at least one pet product or service they had observed or experienced since arriving. Remember, these were American, Danish, and Finnish students, most of whom had never been to Italy before.

To narrow their choices, I asked them to tell me specifically what product they liked so much that they wanted to export it back to their respective home country. Here are their top ten responses:

1. Coffee product with built-in warmer in the bottom of the cup (sold at sporting events)
2. Fresh bread shops
3. Gelato stores (with real Italian ice-cream)
4. Ice-cream automats

5. Video automats
6. Free-standing photo machines
7. Retractable window shutters
8. Ceiling-mounted clothesline rack (for bathrooms)
9. Washbowl for feet
10. Humidifier attachment to radiator

The humidifier is a low-tech product, one of those devices that gets your immediate respect due to its simplicity. It is an elongated vessel for holding water, probably made of ceramic, open at the top with a hook on one side. The hook allows for easy attachment to the tube of a hot-water heat radiator, the kind that used to be common in the U.S. prior to the 1950s. You just fill it with water about once a week and the principle of evaporation goes to work, putting moisture into the air!

. . .

The differences in bed and bathroom fixtures is something that Americans notice right away. For example, the plumbing is quite different than what we are used to in the States. Tourists are often horrified when they go to use the toilet in a public restroom but find that there is no toilet! In fact, in Italy's public restrooms, it is not unusual to find a hole in the floor (sometimes called a "pit") that serves as the commode. Which is not too difficult for men to use, but how do the women do it??

One authority on the subject says the trick is to sort of straddle the thing. You are supposed to put your feet on those groovy porcelain sections encircling the hole and aim at your "target." It is really tricky for a woman wearing slacks, which may explain why most Italian women wear skirts and dresses in public.

Even in people's homes, the toilets are different. I noticed that in the *apartamento* the toilet had no water closet (tank), so I figured it must be inside the wall. Was I ever naïve. Later I learned that there was no water tank at all, but rather high pressure pipes instead that squirt water forcefully into the toilet bowl when flushed, but only for a few seconds. It's not as effective as our system, which releases several gallons of water from the tank, although it is considered more efficient as it uses less water. At least, it is supposed to use less water, in theory.

Now what do I mean by "not as effective?" Let's see, how can I describe this in a delicate way? Well, if you are sitting on the dumper and look straight down into the toilet bowl, you will notice that the water level is very low and off-center. This means that any waste that plops into the toilet bowl (as when doing "number two"), does not go directly into the water! Instead it almost always lands on and clings to the porcelain part of the fixture, just above water level. As you can imagine, that makes the job of flushing the stuff away completely very difficult. One time I had to flush five or six times before it would all go away, thereby consuming many more gallons of water!

. . .

Shower stalls tend to be small and often without curtain or doors to contain the water. The base of the stall may have a ridge no more than an inch or two high so that, with or without a shower curtain, lots of water escapes out into the main part of the bathroom. I guess that's why the hotels always put a drain in the middle of the bathroom floor. Still, I'm not sure I understand the concept. On more than one occasion I had to mop the floor after taking a shower so I would not be standing in water while using a hair dryer! Is this the norm?

Some hotels have an old-fashioned, freestanding bathtub with showerhead and faucet in the middle of the long side of the tub, not at the head of the tub as we are used to. And, again, no shower curtain!

· · ·

Don't plan on a good night's sleep unless you like a firm mattress. The beds in Italy typically have a thin mattress, similar to a rollaway or bunk bed mattress, no box springs but with bowed wooden slats for support instead. A shallow mattress on a wood slat base is very firm, just like the one we had in the apartment. Quite a departure from the big thick mattress and box springs used by Americans. I wonder if anyone has done a comparative study of back problems in different countries?! (If so, I bet the Italians have *fewer* back maladies than we do.)

As for the hotel beds in Italy, the mattresses there were often thicker (with tourists in mind?), and many consisted of two twin mattresses shoved together—like a king size bed with a crack in the middle.

· · ·

Turning our attention to the topic of shopping etiquette, the do's and don'ts of dealing with people in the shops, stores and supermarkets of Italy, here are eight tips to guide you through the maze.

1. Don't try to shop during the lunch hour, and don't try to eat when it's time to shop.

Imagine what it would be like if you could shop only on certain days of the week, and certain times of the day! And to confuse things further, not all stores and restaurants would adhere to the same schedule, so you would have to remember which ones are open when. At lunch time, all the stores might be closed so that during your lunch hour you have no choice but to go somewhere and eat, because that is when the restaurants are open! Or, on Sundays, even though you may not feel like staying at home, the stores and restaurants are closed! Well, that's the way it is in Italy today, for the most part.

A good example is the day Gloria and I took the train to Venice, which happened to be Thanksgiving Day in the USA. We started out early in the morning and arrived in Venice at 3:00 P.M. when the restaurants were all closed. We had had nothing to eat all day and were famished. We were also feeling sorry for ourselves because we knew the rest of the family back home was feasting on turkey and dressing, sweet potatoes, and pumpkin pie! Nonetheless, our search was futile because the restaurants would not reopen until 7:00 P.M. So, we had to settle for a banana. But, that's another story.

On Sundays, just about everything is closed. Except for the *pizzerias,* which are allowed to open on Sunday nights but must shut down on Monday. I recall a Sunday morning when I got up, dressed and went out, determined to find a place where I could sit and enjoy a nice hot cup of coffee and a *briosche.* After walking all over the neighborhood, I did find one place that was open for lunch, but they said they were not serving coffee! Amazing! I left, walked another six blocks to catch a bus, then rode to the train station, which I knew had a snack bar open 24/7.

• • •

2. Patronize the little shops, and get to know the shopkeepers.

One of the delightful things about Italy is the variety of little shops in every neighborhood where you can find what you need and get to know the owner-manager on a personal level. Italy is still largely a country of shopkeepers. And it is really neat to explore the different shops that specialize in one thing or another. For example: there is the *macelleria* (that sells just meats), the *paneteria* (bread), the *gelateria* (ice cream), the *pasticceria* (delicious pastries and candies). And the shops are run by the people who own them. The second time you go in, they remember you and what you bought the first time you were there. It's spooky!

There are also some supermarkets and shopping malls in Italy but very few. In Torino, for example, one mall has a large superstore (much like a K-Mart) that carries both general merchandise and food, and a variety of mall shops that feature apparel, food, electronics, toys, and jewelry. This particular mall was very busy when I was there, and there was much concern about what impact it might have on the neighborhood shops. I could understand the concern because this new competition could ruin one of the most charming and characteristic features of the Italian landscape. Next time I visit Italy I don't want to see all cookie-cutter malls and Mc Donald's like we have over here. If that's the case, I might as well stay home!

. . .

3. Don't try it on for size unless you intend to buy it.

You have to use discretion when you go into a store and ask to try on a dress, a sweater, a suit, or some other item of clothing. My experience, and that of some of the students, was that the salesperson may get quite upset if you try something on and then don't buy!

Now, how are you supposed to know if you like something until you try it on?! I think maybe the Italian merchant feels a personal bond with his merchandise. And if you get too familiar with it (by touching or trying it on), and then rejecting it, maybe they take that as a personal insult? If you really want to stir things up, try on 8–10 items, and then tell them you are not interested!

. . .

4. Don't plan on returning your purchase.

When you buy a shirt, a skirt, shoes, or other merchandise in Italy, it is presumed that you will use the item or dispose of it in some way to your satisfaction, but that you will not—I repeat, NOT—return it to the store.

Once you have bought it, it is yours and the people running the store do not ever want to see it again!

In some countries, like England, consumers engage in a phenomenon called *deshopping* that has become quite popular. Deshopping is the deliberate return of goods for reasons other than faults in the product, and in its pure form it is premeditated. This means that people often buy stuff knowing full well that they will return it later, after getting some use out of it (like a prom dress or a music CD). Of course, this only works in situations where the vendor has a liberal return policy, which is not the case in Italy. I saw a woman try to return a lace tablecloth because it appeared to be soiled. She was told that she should have inspected the item *before* purchasing it, not afterwards.

. . .

5. Plan to do some outside shopping.

Another fun thing about shopping in Italy is the experience of the open-air market, which is popular in cities and towns throughout the country (it reminded me of Cincinnati's Findlay Market where my grandpa shopped at least once a week back in the good old days).

There were two open-air markets near the apartamento, one a block away in Piazza Guala (open Tuesday, Thursday, and Saturday mornings), the other and much larger one a couple of miles away in Piazza Bengazi, and open almost every day of the week. I was amazed at the variety and assortments of items they sell, not only fresh fruits and vegetables, but also apparel, toys, toiletries, jewelry, housewares, and sundries, all from portable stalls set up and operated by the vendors. Jera and Mark had advised me that you can get some really good bargains at the open-air market, and they were right. For example, umbrellas and pajamas cost $10–$20 compared with $40–$60 and up at the downtown stores.

At the risk of offending my Asian friends, let me caution you to examine closely anything you think about buying from street vendors and open-air markets. They tend to have a lot of merchandise that is made in China. In fact, I once chided (in my best Italian) a vendor for selling toys made in China instead of ones made in Italy. I mean, after all, if I wanted to buy "MADE IN CHINA," I would go to China. Or just stay at home in the USA where almost everything comes from China these days! The vendor appeared indifferent to my concern.

• • •

6. Don't touch the bananas!

The same principle of caution seems to apply to bananas. So, now I am warning you in advance. Do not, I repeat—DO NOT EVER touch the bananas (or any other produce, for that matter), unless you are in a self-serve store like a supermarket.

Gloria and I had our encounter with the banana the day we were in Venice, where all the restaurants were closed. Walking along cobblestone alleyways, we discovered, to our delight, a produce store. Gloria suggested that we buy a couple of bananas to tide us over. Well, I walked over to the banana table in the far corner of the store and proceeded to pick out what I thought were a couple of ripe ones. All hell broke loose! The woman tending the store rushed over and grabbed the bananas from my hands while yelling "*Non tocare! Non tocare!*" She didn't even have to say *Non tocare* (Don't touch) because I got the message from her gestures and tone of voice. Since returning from our trip, we have had at least two other persons relate almost identical experiences!

• • •

7. You may need an interpreter to shop at the supermarket.

One day I left school early because I wanted to stop at the neighborhood supermarket by the name of PAM on the way home to buy a mop. It happened to be a Wednesday. That was when I discovered the supermarkets are closed on Wednesday afternoons! Tradition, I guess.

One of the first things you notice upon entering PAM is how all the shopping carts are chained together. To use one, you must insert a coin into the slot of a little box attached to the handle of a cart. This releases it from the chain. After returning your cart and rechaining it, the coin automatically pops back out. This ensures that customers will return carts to the place they belong if they want their money back. The result: no stray carts out in the parking lot and no need to have store employees spend time collecting carts!

The PAM is small by our standards, about 8,000 to 10,000 square feet of floor space. Its unusual features include the following:

- A salad bar, 90% of which was devoted to olives. Nine bins of olives, plus one other item!
- A nice assortment of food products like cheeses, hams, salamis, peppers, olive oil, coffee (*Lavazza*), candies, desserts, and pastries.
- Olives in a plastic pouch (on the shelf, not refrigerated); as well as in jars and bulk. Italians prefer to buy fresh olives sold in bulk, I am told.
- Radishes in a clear plastic pouch shaped like a root; really cute!
- An interesting assortment of beers, wines, and liquors. Lots of scotches, some vodka, tequila, gins, lots of brandies, liquors, and cordials; but

very little bourbon or blends! Only Four Roses and a brand called Blackland Whiskey, the latter being a cheap, sweet-tasting booze that was really nasty (yes, I tried it). No Jack Daniels, although I did see JD in some of the bars.
- A few recognizable American brands, like Kleenex, Colgate, Coke, and 7-Up. Even a can of premixed Four Roses and Coke! Kind of a neat product concept.
- For bathing, body shampoo is more prevalent than bar soap. Trying to decipher shampoo and conditioner products was another challenging experience. I wanted to avoid buying body shampoo for my hair, or dog shampoo for my body!
- Fresh eggs, in cartons, stacked in the middle of the floor, not refrigerated! Once again we asked Mark if he knew why the food stores don't refrigerate their eggs, especially with the dangers of harmful bacteria.

As always, Mark came through:

I just spoke to Charlie in the bar and he said that by law in Italy it is not necessary to refrigerate eggs. All the stores that I have been in don't refrigerate the eggs. The problem in the U.S. is they probably shoot the chickens up with so many hormones.

Gloria said to be sure to mention that the eggs over there are fresh and wonderful, nothing like the pathetic excuses for eggs we have back home. Even the color is different—the yolks are more of a deep orange. The eggs we enjoyed in Greece were equally extraordinary!

• • •

8. Hide your small bills when paying at the checkout.

Ready to pay up and check out? Listen carefully. They do not want your larger bills. In fact, they will grab the change right out of your hand! Once I tried to give the cashier a large bill but she saw that I also had in my hand some smaller denominations, which she just reached out and grabbed from me, saying, "You have it, right here!" Very pushy! The best strategy if you want to hold on to some small change for emergencies is to hide the smaller stuff and show only the big bills.

• • •

The Italian consumer has a diverse array of choices though often quite different than the ones we are used to. Perhaps it should not be surprising if the same principle applies to the food and the cuisine. "Italian" food in Italy is not the same as "Italian" food in America.

13

WHAT! YOU DON'T LIKE THE FOOD?

Everything you see, I owe to spaghetti.
—Sophia Loren (b. 1934)

Playwright Neil Simon said it best (according to a TV Travel Channel quotation): "There are two great truths in the universe: (1) the law of gravity, and (2) everybody loves Italian food."

Now I wonder what kind of Italian food he was talking about, Italian-American food or Italian-Italian food? It is my contention that the stuff brought to America and preserved here by the Italians who migrated years ago represents the essence of *authentic Italian cooking*. In contrast, the food that is made in Italy today by the people who never left, I refer to this as *revisionist Italian cuisine*.

We know that those who left Italy were the smart ones because they were our forefathers. They gave to us, the second- and third-generation descendents, unheard-of opportunities to live in a free country where the sky is the limit. For their foresight and courage and adventuresome spirit, we are eternally grateful.

As for those who stayed behind, why did they stay? Maybe they were better off, or less adventurous, or otherwise lacking in motivation to relocate. Maybe the Italians who never left Italy hung around so they could change the recipes after the others emigrated to the USA and other parts of America. Or maybe they just forgot to keep a copy of the recipes? Who knows?

Anyway, here is what I think happened. I believe that our grandparents and great-grandparents brought the real thing with them when they came over here. We know that. They brought the recipes and preserved the real Italian cuisine, passing it on from generation to generation. Since everyone loved it, Italian-American restaurants sprang up all over the place and the people came. Sure, once in awhile the cook would throw in a new twist and try to make it better. But they are on the whole the same authentic dishes brought here from the Old Country. Now, when you go visit Italy today, what you find over there is something completely different! Why?

When I first thought about this, I said maybe this is just a theory that sounds good but is obviously facetious. Then I decided to include it in the book anyway, just to stir things up. I did some further research and found to my amazement that there are other people who actually agree with this line of thinking. Wherever I discuss this subject—at cocktail parties, family gatherings, on street corners, in the men's room—most people say, "Yes, I think that is what happened! *E' vero!*"

Another reason I know this is more than theory is because I studied the history of Italian assimilation into the American culture. It is well-documented that Italians were the first immigrant group to retain their own ethnic foods after arriving in the USA instead of adapting to the Anglo-

Saxon fare of mainstream Americana. (In fact, for more on this point, see the Travel Channel video by Burt Wolf on "Italian Food in America.")

That is why Italian food became so popular here in the first place! Now, when we of Italian ancestry return to Italy, it is only to discover that they have changed the food on us. It is different! Did they think we wouldn't notice?!

. . .

I wanted to engage in a dialogue about this subject with some real Italians, just to see what they would say, but since I could not find any nearby, I did the next best thing and did more research. I uncovered a Professor Mangoni of the Second University of Naples who has been busy doing research into the origins and authenticity of pizza. In a *Wall Street Journal* article, he was quoted as saying that the goal of his project is to create standards for what constitutes "real" pizza.

The article is a little sketchy as to Professore Mangoni's precise requirements for real pizza, but he does give an example of how a pizza margherita is made in his restaurant: A layer of tomato paste on top of the dough, then gobs of mozzarella, then fresh tomatoes and basil. He says it's important to separate the mozzarella from the starch in the dough. Also, you have to use a particular kind of mozzarella called *mozzarella di bufala campania*. He says you can use either basil or oregano, but not both! Mixing the two, Professor Mangoni says, is "abominable!"

Not surprisingly the professor does not have a high regard for pizzas covered with bean sprouts, Roquefort cheese, pineapple, or hot fudge. He says that's not pizza. Or, how about a pizza topped with lemon cream, amaretto cookies, powdered sugar, chocolate and orange sauce (a pizza of that description actually won top honors one year at the convention of the Milan-based Association of Pizza Chefs!)? The professor says, "If people want to make pizzas with pineapple, that's fine with me. But they can't call them Neapolitan pizzas." I wonder what he would say about the pizza with French fries on top that you find in some parts of Italy today!

Another expert who I'm sure would be quick to take issue with the Carusone theory of Italian food is Antonio Pace, the head of the True Neapolitan Pizza Association. He might be even harder to convince than the Professor. "Pizza," he says, "was born in Naples," which, of course, is true. So far, so good.

But, then he goes on to say that "no other pizza exists. Contraband attempts to make pizza Roman, or even Japanese, are only imitations of or deviations from Neapolitan pizza." Can you believe it? His comment is a slap in the face of some of his own countrymen, the people of Rome, and he puts them in the same category as the Japanese! This is a typical Italian ploy!

As for Italian-American pizza, Mr. Pace believes that "pizza was brought to the USA by someone who wasn't a real pizza chef. Whoever it was," he says, "he made pizza *his* way, not the original way." What he overlooks, however, is the fact that pizza was brought to the USA by the common people of Naples and Campania province, and from Sicily, people who made pizza in their homes; not from some commercial pizzeria in the back alleys of *Napoli*. In fact, I have serious doubts that Mr. Pace has ever been to the USA, as I have never seen him here!

Phyllis Macchioni, on the other hand, is obviously an intelligent woman and astute observer of the Italian scene because her views and mine are quite similar. An editor for *The Informer* magazine, she wrote an excellent article entitled "Italians" several years ago. I believe she would be quick to agree with my viewpoint about the food. Why? Because she talks about the strong feelings Italian Americans have for Italy and for their heritage. In fact, she says she believes that "Italo-Americans are more Italian than the Italians." Aha! Put that on your pizza and eat it, Professor Mangoni!

. . .

When I returned from a three-month sabbatical in California back in the 1980s (my first visit to the West Coast), people asked what I liked best about California. I answered without hesitation—"The food." But, the same is not true of my visit to Italy! Having been raised on Italian food while growing up in Ohio, it never occurred to me that Italian-American food and Italian-Italian food would be so different. Which leads to another touchy question.

How can you say you don't like the food? Do you go to someone's home, accept their hospitality, enjoy their company, and then after you leave tell everyone you didn't like their food? Of course not! So, it is a little awkward to write a book like this in the first place, of course. I mean, what if I decide to go back someday? Will I have to change my name?

No, I cannot really say that I did not like the food, but I can say that it is different and that some of it looked or sounded unappealing. I was once told by a successful businessman and friend from Greece that he thought the Americans had taken Italian food and made it better! Mark's Italian wife, Rafaella, had told us about her two-year stay in New York, and how she did not like the Italian-American food. Another affirmation of how different these kinds of things really are for each of us.

One of the first things you will notice is that Italians often use lots of heavy sauces, oils, fats, and seafood. If you are a seafood lover, that's a good thing. As for me, I can honestly say that I do like many kinds of fish and seafood, but I like it to be cooked! And not eyeballing me from my plate!

One night I had swordfish that was not fully cooked, just lightly singed. Another time I had something called

"Fish in a Tent" (it was baked inside a raised wrap of aluminum foil). When I went to uncover the fish, it looked as if they had just taken it out of the water and plopped it right on my plate, eyes wide open looking up at me! And it had so many skeletal bones from head to tail that eating it was a delicate and unsightly experience.

Gloria and I had a plate of *gnocchi* in Florence that was mushy but yet tasted uncooked. We argued with the manager about it and he insisted that it is supposed to be mushy, and not *al dente*. "GNUKKI" is what I called it!

Another food that's not too appealing to the American palate is the prunes. Italians eat a lot of prunes, which are supposed to be good for you because they flush fats out of the system. Italians feed prunes to the tourists every morning for breakfast (*prima colazione*), and I also saw them used as a topping on a roast. I ate a few myself and they were not that bad going down.

There were a great many things, however, that I did not try because they did not sound good to me. Is it fair to be critical of food you did not even try? I'll let you be the judge of that.

Most of the items on my list of foods that turned me off are not dishes, as such, but rather ingredients that make up various dishes that may be known by different names. So, just because the name of a dish sounds okay, that doesn't mean you will be happy with what you get. For example, when is the last time you ate some frog soup, or pigs' ears, or offal? (I don't even know what *offal* is, but you have to admit it sounds awful, doesn't it?) See what you think.

- "*Costoletta alla Milanese*"—Many people love this dish. It is like a breaded veal cutlet, similar to Austrian Wiener schnitzel, I think. It might have been very good but I was afraid it would not be well-cooked (*ben cotto*).

- "R*isotto di Secoli*"—a rice dish made with butcher's leftovers
- hare stew
- frog soup
- *offal*
- lamb's innards
- oxtail
- octopus
- chopped anchovies
- sliced white truffles
- chicken livers
- tripe
- pork stew with ribs, trotters, crackling and pig's ear
- stuffed pigs' trotters
- *Mortadella* ("dead meat," same as *Bologna* sausage)
- Use of lard sometimes instead of olive oil
- pigs' feet
- chicken giblets
- mutton paste
- eel and sturgeon
- mussels
- oysters
- black rice made with ink from the squid
- cold fish
- pigeon
- snails
- chopped pigs liver
- wild boar
- jugged hare

See anything you like? Or have you lost your appetite? Maybe it's all what you get used to?! Maybe some of it is really good but I will never know.

Or maybe I am not being fair to the Italians. After all, other ethnic groups in Europe and elsewhere have their share of "yummy" dishes, don't they? Take England, for example, which the Italians for some strange reason refer to as *Inghilterra* (EEN-GIL-TARE'-AH). England is not a country exactly known for its cuisine, or even for decent food, such as:

Blood Pudding—-More like a sausage, it is made from pig blood boiled with meal and seasoning and stuffed in a casing. You slice it and fry it and eat it for breakfast! This is a real British delight. They not only like it, they love it!

Haggis—a Scottish dish made of suet and minced sheep lungs, hearts and livers. YUK! (No wonder they have to wear kilts! HAHAHA!!!)

. . .

My friend, Mark, somehow got the impression that I did not like the food.

> *What do you mean you didn't like the food? How can you not like the food? It's the best in the whole world. That's how I got up to 200 pounds!*

I told him not to think that there was nothing I liked. In fact, there was a lot of food I really, really liked. For example:

- The Pizza—especially *Napolitan* pizza like I enjoyed in Caserta.
- *Bel Paese* cheese—a smooth, soft cheese with a delicate taste from Lombardy, and difficult to find here in the States.
- *Carciofatto*—artichoke hearts in a jar including about an inch of the tender inner leaves as well

as the heart, marinated in olive oil and spices; substantial and succulent. Mmmmmm!
- *Briosche*—A croissant stuffed with fruit or chocolate. This is the most popular breakfast food in Italy, taken with *caffe o cappuccino*. Wonderful, especially hot out of the oven!
- *Prosciutto*—an Italian ham
- G*elato*—The ice cream is great! I would say this was the students' favorite Italian food. Although, as our friends, the McConvilles aptly pointed out... where's the spumoni?
- Penne Pasta *Arrabiata*—al dente. (*Arrabiata* means angry!) This is a spicy tomato sauce. At Noe Pizzaria, the penne was perfectly cooked, always *al dente*! I asked the chef for the secret and learned that the quality of the pasta varies, depending on the water where it was made. He said to always look for pasta with the longest cooking time. If you can choose between pasta that takes 10 minutes to cook and another 14 minutes, always buy the latter. But, be sure to remove it from the water after no more than 14 minutes. Don't buy cheap pasta that cooks in only four or five minutes.
- Panzarotti—a fried cheese-filled crescent, like a small calzone only deep fried. Consists of a homemade dough filled with sauce, mozzarella cheese, homemade sausage, onions, mushrooms, and pepperoni, sometimes baked to a golden brown instead of fried. The one I ate was cheese-filled, hot, and delicious.

Of course, the two ingredients that make Italian food so good, olive oil and garlic, are popular in other Mediterranean countries as well, and research has proven them to be healthy ingredients. Garlic is said to be good for your heart, and olive oil is low in cholesterol. In fact, a reference I ran across in the *Culture Shock* book talks about the mixing effects of oil and alcohol: "The oil in the food tends to counteract the effects of the alcohol." Interesting. Now you can eat more and drink more. *Salute!*

. . .

To the credit of the Italians, I should point out that Italy is considered to have the best food in Europe, certainly better than the French. Consider, for example, this commentary on Italian and French food by Arturo Barone, who wrote the famous book on *Italians First!*

> *Indeed, anyone who frequents restaurants as a matter of course, knows only too well that, at least as far as London is concerned, Italian or even Chinese or other restaurants provide better food than the French.*

. . .

If the food was a surprise, then the music and entertainment scene in Italy was a shock. I was looking for traditional Italian music, dancing, and celebration. It wasn't there. Did I look in the wrong places? Did I spend too much time in the North, and not enough in the South? Did I turn in too early at night?

As you may recall, I enjoyed two nightclub experiences in Rome (the Derby and the secret hideaway place). I also enjoyed the wine *festa* in Asti on a Sunday afternoon, and the *palio di asini* and truffle festa in Alba on another Sunday. But that was it! As enjoyable as these places were, none of them had the kind of traditional entertainment I expected.

I thought surely the restaurants would have live music, or at least recordings of soft violins and romantic Italian ballads. WRONG! With one or two exceptions, the restaurants and "bars" I visited played either blaring rock music from a small radio, or they played no music at all. In the pubs and nightclubs, with one or two exceptions, I generally encountered raucous disco sounds, and sounds that reminded me of Latino rock.

In Sorrento, a place advertised *"Tarantella and Traditional Italian Musica."* Since Sorrento is a popular tourist area, I got my hopes up when I saw the ad in a local magazine, thinking that they must be trying to appeal to visitors like me. Gloria and I searched for the place during the daytime to check it out. Well, it was difficult to find, but we finally succeeded. We kept walking back and forth across a busy intersection in the vicinity of the address but did not see it. Finally, we asked someone for directions, and only then found it on the lower level of a building around the corner.

When we returned that evening at around 10:00 P.M., the place was open but totally empty and there was no music. The doorman said to come back at around 11:00, saying that they would have traditional music and dancing at *le undici* (eleven o'clock). So, we did. And, guess what? The place was still deader than a doornail! This time he said to come back still later, after midnight. Well, we decided that this was not a hopeful sign, so we gave up and went back to our hotel.

I really think there is a void here, a great opportunity for an entrepreneurial business venture, to present traditional Italian music and dancing in Italy (sounds crazy, doesn't it?). Not just for the tourists, mind you, but for the local population as well. I mean, what's wrong with these Italians anyway?! Don't they like the traditional stuff anymore? Or did they change the music along with the food? Maybe the younger generation is trying too much to be American.

. . .

In Torino the students attended the discos that were down near the river, establishments that did not open until midnight. These were dumpy-looking places located in a not-so-nice neighborhood. Maybe okay for groups of young people looking to party, but not for me. One of the students, in fact, had his watch stolen off his arm at one of these places.

I mention this aspect of Italian life in a fax to my then still-single son, Tony:

> *I have thought about what it would be like to be young and single in Italy. The "bars" here are not at all like our bars. And the girls do not date unless properly introduced through family or friends.*

The year after my return, Mark kept me informed of the activities of the new crop of students, like the time they all went to a soccer match between Juventus (the Torino team) and Manchester United from England. Juventus won, 1–0, and the students really loved the match. Mark also reported on some extracurricular activities the students had engaged in that same day.

> *The only crisis we had was when some of the students went out in the afternoon before the match to party. They ran into a bunch of English near Porta Nuova and when they were drinking at the bar, one of the English guys told one of our students to open his bottle of Heineken with his teeth. Well, upon doing this he cracked his tooth in half...the student happened to be from Ohio...from Miami of Ohio. Are they that dumb over at Miami of Ohio?*

. . .

Surfing the Internet one day while reworking this chapter, I ran across an Italian website by the name of "Live Music at Night." Wow, I thought, now I can uncover all the good places that have music and dancing that I missed. The website included 17 establishments in five cities: Caserta, Como, Napoli, Roma, and Venezia (Venice). Three of the establishments simply listed a name and address, with no further information. Another three were primarily restaurants with extensive menus but said nothing about music. Another two were described as *birrerie*. A *birreria*, according to Mark, differs from a bar, which also serves beer and other alcoholic drinks but is primarily a place where the Italians go to drink coffee in the morning or grab something quick to eat. The *birreria* does not usually open early in the morning like a bar, and the bar does not stay open late in the evening like the *birreria* does.

The two birrerie said nothing about music. Remember, we were searching here for *traditional* Italian music.

Two of the remaining nine said they had music, but that's all they said. Another four identified a particular genre of music (none of which was what we were looking for) and gave no indication as to whether it was live or recorded. One of these featured jazz, one alternative music, another billed itself as a disco pub, and the fourth offered karaoke! Now we were down to three possibilities of the original 17.

All three of these places featured live bands: the Black Crow in Como, an English Pub with a beer garden, that featured rock, rock blues, non-solo rock, country rock, pop rock, cover rock, and rock-n-blues, everything but traditional Italian music.

Next, in Napoli, there was the Lido Pola Club, in a beautiful location on the bay. This Club's bands play disco, cabaret, rock, dance, and acid funky soul italiano (whatever that is!). Again, no traditional or classic Italian *musica*!!

Finally, we found Riot, also in Napoli. Here, the bands played blues, cover rock, acid-hip hop, jazz, Latino Americana, World Music, disco, and, oh, yes—on about three nights per month—they play some *Musica Italiana* or *Musica Napoletana Classica*. I will believe it when I see it. Also, they have a special tourist menu every Sunday morning along with live music for about U.S. $12.

Wouldn't you think that at least in the popular tourist cities of Florence, Venice, and Rome there would be some traditional entertainment? And not just on a Sunday morning! An interesting aside: regardless of the entertainment, all these establishments served food. In fact, it appeared that any place that served alcohol in Italy also served food; if not full meals, then at least appetizers and sandwiches. The concept of "drinking" as well as the concept of eating, is quite different there.

. . .

To be fair, I must point out that other travelers did not have the same disappointing experience that I did with regard to the entertainment (or even the food). Shortly after they arrived in Italy, Professor Bob (who succeeded me as the SAA Visiting Professor) and his wife, Loraine, for example, found a celebration with traditional music in a small Alpine village, an area outside my itinerary. Bob emailed me a description of an encounter they had while driving through the mountains.

> *The first week we toured the small villages in the Italian Alps. We just couldn't get enough of the scenery. In one small village we went for a walk after dinner in the hotel. We heard music playing and followed it to a small park where they were having a local celebration. It was a wonderful local band with accordions and other instruments and great singers. We met an English-speaking*

> *woman from the Philippines who was married to an Italian, and soon we were part of their group of friends. We wished we hadn't eaten as they were roasting huge slabs of beef ribs and sausages on giant grills. We danced and listened to music until midnight when we tore ourselves away.*
>
> *In another small village, we went to a Parasol museum that was fascinating. The town has been known for making and repairing umbrellas since the early 1800s. We've enjoyed many meals at sidewalk cafes. The pasta and breads are incredible.*

When I first read this, I was more than a little envious since it sounded like the kind of thing I would have truly enjoyed. "What right did they have," I asked myself, "to find such a neat place?! Ha! But, hey, I had a great time! I have no regrets. I made the choice not to drive but to rely solely on public transportation, and I loved that aspect of Italy, especially the trains.

If one wants to visit small towns off the beaten track, however, and especially in the mountains, a *machina* (auto) is a necessity. I was able to take day trips by train to Asti and Alba, both small towns south of Torino, because they happen to be on a rail line.

• • •

The trains afforded me various side-trips to Switzerland, Germany, and Austria. Each trip was entertainment in itself since I loved watching the changing scenery of the passing countryside, witnessing the aesthetic and cultural differences in the cities, and comparing the varying levels of customer service in the stores. (After Gloria arrived, she and I also enjoyed a whirlwind weekend trip to Greece.)

Swiss food was similar to Italian—-nothing original—because I was mainly in the Italian sector. But the presentation of both food and entertainment had more of an American flair, and the stores and services were geared more to a tourist population.

It is interesting to note that there really are no Swiss people, per se, they are either German, French or Italian! In fact, the Swiss are not very popular among the Italians due to the fact that during World War II Switzerland was neutral. Thus, according to the Italians, the Swiss just sat on the fence and benefited at the expense of the other countries in the region.

In Austria, I enjoyed an excellent Wiener schnitzel. In Germany, I ate the best hamburger I have ever tasted. It was almost like a piece of meatloaf in the shape of a small football, juicy and succulent. Mmmmm! The bars in Germany actually have bar stools with people sitting on them, drinking beer from big mugs and talking to each other. Also, it was not too difficult to find some traditional German music in Munich.

Actually, the six-day rail trip through Switzerland, Germany, and Austria was a story unto itself as I wound up traveling with one of the female students in the program as her companion. As you might imagine, this raised some eyebrows back home, and called for considerable explanation and backpedaling on my part! I will explain more about this later, in Chapter 17.

14

BUREAUCRACY ITALIAN STYLE

It is a different Italy than I had dreamed of all my life, not this miserable, poverty-stricken, humiliated Italy we see now, governed by the dregs of the nation.
—Garibaldi (in 1881, a year before his death)

An Italian entrepreneur says her government makes it unreasonably complicated for new businesses to get started. She says all she wanted to do is write and publish a small newsletter.

First she discovered that you must have a *Direttore Responsabile* who is registered with the journalists' association. "The paperwork was incredible, including a copy of my criminal record from Rome and a document verifying my being a registered voter. They had no interest whatsoever in my ability to write; they merely needed the correct documentation."

After all that, she still could not publish the newsletter until she went to the Tribunale to have a number assigned to her by the courthouse. That took another three months! Only then was she legally able to proceed with her new business.

This is a chapter about red tape. It's about how things in Italy work and often don't work. It's about government, politics, taxes, and bureaucracy—Italian style.

. . .

Every country has its share of governmental inefficiencies and lack of responsiveness to citizen needs. So, why is Italy so often singled out as the worst in this arena?

Well, for starters and at the heart of the Italian bureaucracy is what some have called "the most complex tax and legal system in the world." Some of the laws on the books actually go back to the days of the Roman Empire!

Another factor stems from Italy's liberal social spending programs, including pension, maternity leave, vacation benefits, and other social welfare outlays that raise taxes and inflate prices. Still, when compared with other EU countries, welfare spending in Italy does not appear to be excessive. The one account in which Italy spends a lot more is pensions: Italy 15.4% (of Gross Domestic Product), Germany 12.1%, France 12.7%. The EU average is 11.9%. Italy is especially low in spending on health and family, the latter being understandable since in Italy family takes care of its own.

Another thing that seems to come into play here is the deep-rooted antagonism between the populace and the civil service employees. Citizens must endure annoying and frustrating rituals, as when dealing with the post office, the telephone company, and even the private banking sector. Also, the entanglements involved in trying to get a visa, driver's license, marriage license, the right to own a TV, or simply finding a place to live are truly absurd.

When you buy a television set in Italy, for example, the shopkeeper is obliged to report your name and address to RAI, the national broadcasting agency. Every year thereafter, you must pay a TV tax, called a *canone* (not *cannoli*!) of roughly $100 per family, regardless of the number of TVs.

Once your name is "in the system," it is very difficult to avoid paying the *canone*, whether you still own a TV set or not, and even if you never watch it. One man received a letter from RAI asking why he did not have a TV license in his name, given that he had a subscription to Pay TV. (Aha! Obviously they cross-check to track down deadbeats.) The answer the man gave was that his family's *canone* was in his wife's name, which was true.

The Italian government has estimated that the citizens of Italy pay about 45 percent of their income to taxes of one form or another. Other sources suggest that there is a substantial reservoir of unpaid taxes, and that Italians are quite adept at tax avoidance, much more so than in other Western countries.

. . .

The Italian Constitution boldly protects mothers, children, and the young. It says that workplace conditions must allow the working woman to fulfill her "essential family function." The intent is to protect the working mother and her baby before and after birth, as well as during periods of illness through the baby's early childhood.

A pregnant employee is obliged to leave her job two months before she is due and to stay away for three months afterwards. During that time, she is paid 80 percent of her salary. Following this five-month mandatory leave, a six-month optional maternity leave is available, at 30 percent of salary. After that, the mother becomes entitled to her vacation days, which are fully paid and count for another month. At that point, after one year, she returns with her job intact.

Recent changes in the law now allow for the six-month optional leave to be split between mother and father! During baby's first year, for example, daily periods of rest from work are available to either parent.

• • •

Another area of government intrusion into the market concerns the regulation of retail sales. Do you want to put merchandise on sale in your own store? Well, it may or may not be permitted, according to an article in *The Informer*.

> *"Sales" in Italy are fairly strictly defined. We (British and Americans) tend to call everything "sales," but there are in fact three types of special offers under Italian law: saldi (sales as we understand them); vendite promozionali (special promotions); and liquidazioni (closedown sale). Each is subject to particular rules.*
>
> *Saldi, which are strictly for fashion or seasonal products, may be held twice a year, only during a two-month period at the end of summer, and a two-month period at the end of winter. Special rules govern the other two types of sales, including the type of merchandise, posting of prices, and length of the sale.*

• • •

Although Italian citizens do not have a high regard for government, or for authority of any kind, voting is nonetheless taken very seriously and is regarded as a civic duty.

Ninety percent of the people vote! Compare that with the low proportion of voters in America and in other European elections. Compare it with Rudolph Giuliani's election to a second term as mayor of New York City, which had a voter turnout of only 33 percent! Shame on *l'America*!

. . .

According to the tourist books, government office hours in Italy are 8:30 A.M. to 1:45 P.M., Monday through Friday. I asked Mark if he knew anything about this and, as usual, he seemed to have a little knowledge and a lot of opinion. This is what he told me:

> *It is safe to say that one deals with employees who lack a motivation to provide a service that their job descriptions entail. These people lack the motivation in the sense that they have a job for life, a job they acquired by knowing somebody, and there is an overall lack of formal training.*
>
> *The "job for life" concept is something that is deeply ingrained in the culture. Once an employee is hired, it is very difficult to fire the employee. The government places priority on the workers and not on the consumer.*
>
> *To get a civil service job in Italy is many times based on whom you know and not the educational level of the applicant. Government policy requires an exam much like that found in the United States, but priority often is given to the person who has the connections.*

A political movement to dramatically improve government services to the public has emerged. One newspaper labeled the leader of this movement the "Citizen's Champion." The basis of the Plan is that the user should be considered a client, not a victim (That's a good one!). Each agency is to adopt quality standards, simplified procedures, and demonstrate more respect and courtesy. And public offices would have to be open in the afternoon as well as in the morning.

. . .

The first time I walked into the friendly, neighborhood post office, the one near the apartamento in the vicinity of Piazza Guala, what I found there was anything but friendly. "Mio Dio," I thought to myself, "this place is a zoo!"

I had gone there to mail an oversized envelope, which had to be weighed so that I could affix the correct postage. There must have been five or six lines, nay, clusters of people, waiting there for various purposes. So I asked someone where I should go and still wound up getting in the wrong queue.

To make matters worse, people kept cutting into line, people who had just walked in the door. It was chaotic! I asked Mark about this, because I wanted to know if my experience was unique.

That's another example of bureaucracy Italian style! First, we do not know which line to go to because the post office seems to perform many functions other than mail.

Second, just to ask how many francobolli *(stamps) to send a letter or postcard to the States can provide mixed results. Depending on the person you speak with, you will get different prices.*

Third, asking for stamps only to be told that they are out and you have to buy them at a tabaccheria *(a newsstand where they sell tobacco, envelopes, candy, stamps, and sundries)!— whoever heard of going to the post office to buy stamps only to be told that you have to go somewhere else to get them?*

Another curiosity is that nearly all the people pay nearly all their bills through the post office. That's right! To pay Telecom *(the government-owned phone company), Italgas (the Italian gas company), ENEL, or AEM (the electric company), you must pay at the post office. The Italians also pay other bills at the post office: car registration fees, the annual TV canone, and various tax payments.*

On the day the utility bills are due, the post offices are jam-packed with people. You can hear them saying to each other, "I was here before you," or "I am older than you so I should be first." Also, if the post office closes at 5:00 P.M. and you just happen to be in line when the clock hits 4:55 P.M., you are likely to have the window shut on you before you can pay.

Another interesting requirement is that payments at the post office must be in cash. So, all the Italians crammed into the post office to pay bills have their wallets and purses stuffed full of cash. One can only imagine how many have been robbed just going to the post office to satisfy their civic obligations.

Pension checks are paid at the post office too, and in cash. Again, how many of the older people have been robbed coming home from the post office with their monthly pension?

• • •

While e-mailing back and forth on this subject, Mark sent me a message about the post office being closed again unexpectedly, but not due to bureaucratic bungling, or was it?

Peter: Max just came from the post office (Thursday morning at 10:00). It was closed because they were just robbed.

• • •

The Post Office does not have a monopoly on bureaucracy and red tape. The telephone company (TELECOM), also owned and operated by the government, is another "service" organization that often leaves people in a quandary.

The first tip-off that something is wacky is their phone-numbering system. It is baffling. There are seven-digit numbers like we have (not including area code), but there are also eight-digit numbers, six-digit numbers, and even five-digit numbers. Amazing!

For example, there are two different telephone numbers for the school: 639-9254, and 63991. Take your pick! Calling the airlines in Milan, gives you these options:

Continental Airlines	70100102
United Airlines	864831
TWA	77961

What if you have an emergency? Whom do you call? Well, if you look in the phone book under Emergency Phone Numbers, you'd better know something about the jurisdiction of the various police departments. There are at least three listed: *Police, Carabinieri*, and *Vigili Urbani* (Municipal Police). Then, on another list is a number for the *Questura* (Police) station!

. . .

The Telephone Bill. Normally you must accept the telephone company's account of your usage, even when you know for certain that you never could have made half the calls charged to your bill. No complaint would even be considered by the company until the bill being contested had first been paid! Imagine that! "We will let you complain to us but only after you've given us your money." Typical bureaucratic ploy.

Now it is possible to make partial payment of contested bills pending a final decision. Of course, the company still makes you suffer for this enforced courtesy by obliging you to join an endless waiting line in order to first get authorization to complain.

One man decided to challenge two particularly outrageous bills that totaled well over $130 for a phone he said he uses very little. Upon his request, the phone company even installed a special household meter that showed only half the number of *scatti*, or time units, for which they had billed him. However, the company was quick to remind the man that when installing a household meter, only the company's official meter is considered accurate!

. . .

Although Italian trains are generally regarded as a step down from those of other European countries, I thought they were great! Why would anyone want to drive a car when he can sit back, eat, drink, and relax, and watch the beautiful countryside go by? The trains are usually on time, or very close, and reasonably efficient, although on Sunday afternoons and evenings they can be overbooked and chaotic.

Interacting with the conductors can be intimidating—they have the power to make you get off the train. You might recall from Chapter 1 my experience with the conductor who didn't much care for the preprinted 'US'. notation on my Eurailpass. Well, he also made an issue of the way in which I had entered the numbers for that day's date onto my pass. At the time I thought he was being picky, but later realized there was good reason for his concern.

You see, I had simply penned in 7/12 (for December 7th) instead of 07/12. (Remember, Europeans use the day/month/year format, which makes a lot more sense than our month/day/year system). So, what was the big deal?! What was wrong with 7/12?

The big deal is that the way I wrote it is illegal. By leaving out the zero in front of the seven, it opened the door to possible abuse. If someone wanted to try to use that pass again, it would be easy. Just writing 7/12 leaves the option to fill in a one or a two in front of the seven, making it valid also on 17/12, or 27/12.

. . .

One day I went with Mark to the downtown offices of the local transit company to submit the school's requests for student bus passes. Since the bus company offers special rates for students, a staff person must go downtown (il centro) when a new semester starts and fill out a form for each one of the 20 or so new students coming into the program, all of whom are from other countries.

It took awhile to get the proper forms because none of the clerks spoke any English. Then, we moved to a counter, out of the way, and began recording the applicable information from copies of the student passports we had brought with us.

While standing there, we could hear the loud "kabooms" of the clerks pounding their official rubber stamps at the counter behind us. That's when we knew we were witnessing true Italian bureaucracy in action! What we did *not* know was that after nearly an hour of working on these forms, we would be told that on one of the lines we had provided the wrong information. Apparently, we had misunderstood what it was asking!

Peter,

I remember very well and they were asking for date of birth and I thought it said place of birth. This is important because you can't get a student discount if you're older than 25 years old. The question asked about nato *(birth), it asked* nato il - *this means "born when" and* nato a - *means "born where."*

We finally had a nice day but the last week has been raining. It has been really cold and they haven't turned the heat on in the buildings. Remember, they don't turn the heat on until the 15th of Oct. Before that it's against the law.
Ciao.
Mark

• • •

I had only one experience with Italian planes during my trip—on the weekend Gloria and I flew to Greece. We took *ALITALIA* Airlines from the Torino airport to Rome, then on to Athens. The service was reasonably good, although I remember thinking it odd that Italian airlines don't serve alcoholic drinks on domestic flights.

Little did we know at the time how Italians joke about their airline, and what the name, *ALITALIA*, stands for:

> Always
> Late
> In
> Takeoff
> Always
> Late
> In
> Arrival

• • •

Strikes, strikes, and more strikes! I experienced them all. Bus strikes. Train strikes. Plane strikes. And now this! In a news report about the war crimes trial in Rome, families of the Italian men and boys massacred by the

Nazis in 1944 are testifying against former German officers now in their 80s. But the trial's next session may have to be postponed because of a lawyers' strike!

• • •

Many of the functions performed by attorneys in the United States are handled by notaries in Italy. Notaries are public officials appointed for life by the government and are required to have a university degree in law.

Lawyers' compensation in Italy is almost always based on a flat fee. The regulations of the Italian Bar Association do not permit lawyers to accept cases on a contingency or percentage basis.

• • •

One of my most memorable encounters with an Italian bank was when I confronted the dilemma of how to cash a check. I had just found out I was supposed to get some money for doing a seminar at the Torino Chamber of Commerce. In Italy, I was told, you never get paid unless you ask for it!

Actually, I had no intention of asking for it until it dawned on me that the people at the Chamber had never thanked me for doing the seminar. So I decided to call and ask for the money. After much delay, paperwork, and more delay, finally—weeks later—I got paid. But the check they gave me had NONTRANSFERABLE stamped on it. Which meant that I could not sign it over to Jera to cash for me, as I had planned. That led to the next bureaucratic quandary— finding a bank that would cash my check.

The check was drawn on the Banco di San Paulo which is the largest *banco* in Torino. They have branches everywhere. And I had been to the one in my neighborhood before to cash travelers' checks.

The problem is this. You cannot go to any branch of the bank on which a check is drawn to cash it. You must go to the branch where the payer originally opened the account, the address of which is on the face of the check. The bank might have 25 branches in the city but YOU MUST GO TO THE ONE LOCATION THE CHECK IS DRAWN ON!! Can you believe it?

It's not because they don't have computers. So, what is the big deal? Well, I refused to accept such a ridiculous situation and decided to go see for myself.

I went to the neighborhood office of the San Paulo bank, the one I had dealt with before, and asked to see the manager (typical American ploy, eh?). Well, that didn't do any good.

The manager was cordial but firm. When I showed him the check, he said, "You must go to the bank on the check to cash it." I said but in the United States we can cash them at any bank of the same name, like that is the norm, right? Besides, I have no *machina* (car)! He pulled out a map and showed me how to take bus number XX and then transfer to bus number YY.

It was the middle of the day, about an hour before the bank would close. Traffic was terrible. By the time the second bus neared what I thought to be my destination, I was only guessing as to where to get off. I wound up exiting the bus about two blocks too soon, had to run all the way, hoping they would still be open. I made it with barely *cinque minuti* (5 minutes) to spare!

· · ·

Italian bureaucracy is also evident when trying to get a visa, which you must have if you plan to stay more than three months. (Tourists are allowed to visit Italy without a visa for up to three months.)

You can obtain an extended tourist permit for up to a year. You must apply to the local questura (police station), which has almost total discretion as to whether to grant an extension, and for how long! Some people think that maybe your chances are better if the questura does not know you are there!

Under Italian law, every foreigner in Italy is considered a tourist or a resident. Even a tourist planning to stay fewer than three months but more than eight days is supposed to appear in person at the nearest questura within eight days of arrival and to apply for a *Permesso di Soggiorno*. I was advised not to.

. . .

There is the case of an American woman who is temporarily living in Italy to see if she likes it. She thinks she might want to stay and set up a business. So, she decides to gather some information about getting an extended visa.

This is where her problems begin. She cannot get a straight answer from anyone. Not from the local questura, not from the American Consulate in a nearby city, not even from the Italian Consulate in Chicago, her home town. You have to understand that interpretations of visa law and how it applies can vary enormously. Often such matters are deliberately left to the discretion of the local authorities. On top of that, immigration from various countries may be subject to quotas.

There are probably hundreds of Americans living "clandestinely" in Florence and Rome alone. The problem in the case of the woman we are talking about is that she has already made herself visible by declaring her presence to the questura—as required by law. This, of course, increases the risk that the authorities will check on her continued presence in the future.

. . .

Can someone explain to me why we Italians have to make life so complicated for ourselves?

The question is taken from a letter written by an Italian in Florida, USA, and published in the *Corriere della Sera* newspaper. The man was elated to have completed his driving test and obtained an American driver's license, all in the space of seven hours.

By contrast, he says it is incredible what people have to endure to obtain a license in Italy. The application process, the forms you must file, the criteria for passing the test, all the red tape, and then... when you finally get the license, guess what? You have to put a bumper sticker on your car with a big letter 'P' that tells the world that you are *Neopatentato*—-which means you are an amateur, same as an 18-year-old kid who just started driving!

It takes so long to obtain an Italian license because a driving license request involves half the world and his brother: the ACI, the Motorizzazione, the USL, the Prefettura, the Comune, the Courts, and the Ministry of Transport. Not because they all want a say in whether you can drive or not, but because the driver's license, once issued, can be used as a document of identification. There have been changes pending in this area to streamline the process.

• • •

One of the few acceptable reasons for divorce in Italy is separation for a given period of time, a kind of verification that the marriage has effectively broken down.

MINIMUM PERIOD OF SEPARATION
PRIOR TO DIVORCE
3 years with consent
7 years without consent

Other grounds for divorce include a spouse being convicted of certain crimes (e.g., murder, incest, etc.), or for polygamy, or for a sex change.

. . .

Peter,

We have one other thing to tell you. It happened yesterday afternoon and it just proved to me how screwed up this country is sometimes.

You know how the parking is here at the SAA where all the students park on the driveway as you enter the school and also in that one lot in front of the school. Well, there was a car that was partially blocking the entryway to the SAA from Via Ventimiglia. Someone was upset by this so they called the Vigile Urbana (Traffic Police). The Vigile first towed the car and then they noticed a No Parking sign in the parking lot (Can you believe that, there is a "no parking" sign in the parking lot?).

Anyway, they proceeded to give everyone a ticket and I mean everyone who was parked in the school parking lot. The tickets cost about U.S. $35 and everybody was pissed. In fact, the Vigile said that the reason everyone got a ticket was because that one person who was originally parked wrong screwed it up for everyone. That was their justification. Can you believe it? They are crazy!

Mark

15

BUON COMPLEANNO!

Venice is like eating an entire box of chocolate liqueurs in one go.
—Truman Capote (1924–1984), American author

What an incredible moment! After 80 days and 80 nights, there she was, sitting in front of the coffee shop at the Milan airport, right where we arranged to meet. And right on my birthday! Can you believe it?! *Buon Compleanno!*

Gloria says she will always remember the look on my face when she saw me coming down the corridor from the main concourse. I had just caught sight of her and was grinning ear-to-ear. She and I would have time enough to reminisce and share many stories about our separate lives of the preceding weeks. We would have time to hug and kiss and gaze into each other's eyes. We would have time to enjoy a cup of cappuccino before leaving the airport for Torino.

From the day I departed for Italy, Gloria and I knew we would miss each other. As newlyweds, we were still exploring and getting to know each other, doing lots of new and different things together. Still, she had been supportive of my plan to teach in Italy, the original proposal for which long preceded our wedding date. In fact, she delighted in the realization that I could have this once-in-a-lifetime opportunity.

I will never forget a phone conversation, maybe two weeks after arriving in Italy in which Gloria, expressing her melancholy at my absence, said something like, "Maybe we didn't think this through clearly."

I missed the kids and everyone else in the family, too, which caused time to pass more slowly than I had anticipated. Still, all was not lost. My classes, the side trips on those five day weekends, the social activities with Mark, Jera, and the students helped divert my attention from the longing I felt.

Even so, it was often one day at a time as I would look forward to and relish the steady stream of faxes, e-mail, cards, letters, and phone calls from home. My daughter, Nancy, wrote me several beautiful letters that were much appreciated.

In the "yearbook" the students put together at the end of the semester, they asked questions like, "What is the one thing you would have added to your apartment?" Candice, a student from California, said, "Carpeting, a dryer, new couches, VCR, and a thermostat." David, whose nickname was *Cibo* (Food) and who was also from California, said, "Soundproof walls." Alessandra, still another Californian, said, "A heater that works and a washing machine that does not leak." My response: "My wife!"

. . .

The days leading up to Gloria's arrival were filled with anticipation and preparation for the big day. Early in the week I stopped at a floral shop in the neighborhood and placed two orders for flowers, a fresh arrangement for the kitchen table and a fancy bouquet to take to the airport. The apartment had to be scrubbed and cleaned thoroughly, something I had not done since moving in. Oh, sure, I had swept and dusted about every other week, but by now it needed a lot more than that, especially with my wife coming. I even washed the windows, which was no easy task. There were three of them, each consisting of a single huge panel of double-paned glass with Venetian blinds in between. Each window was attached to its frame by horizontal pins at the center, thereby enabling you to swivel them inward and outward from top to bottom.

The day before Gloria was to arrive, on my way to pick up the flowers, I stopped by my favorite *pasticceria* (confectioner) and bought some delicious candies and pastries. These went directly into the tiny *frigorifero* (refrigerator).

I made dinner plans for the Sunday of her arrival when most restaurants would be closed, and checked out the tram and bus schedules needed to get me to the airport and back. Planning the transportation was probably more complicated than anything. At Mark's urging, I had actually entertained the notion of renting a car for the occasion, but two minutes later decided against it. I thought it would be more fun to be able to relax and chat with Gloria on the bus, not to worry about my driving. Besides, having seen Italian driving, I had no desire to participate in that bloodthirsty sport. Hey, I had survived eleven weeks without driving in Italy and saw no reason to start now.

So, I did some research and became informed about the schedules and connections of trams and buses to get me to the airport. I did not want any last-minute surprises. With Mark's help I was able to verify timetables and identify precise locations of the tram stops to take me downtown, then from the intercity bus terminal to the airport. I studied and restudied the map of Torino to see how everything was going to fit together, and how far I would have to walk to make connections.

As if that—and teaching classes—were not enough to keep me busy, I was also working on an itinerary for the 28 days Gloria and I would be together. Monica, a travel agent whose office is on *Via Genova* near the school, helped me book hotels in various cities and order airline tickets for a weekend trip to Greece. We already had our Eurail passes, which must be purchased before leaving the States.

Early in the week I completed and sent home a copy of the itinerary (below) so the family would know our whereabouts at any given time. I especially wanted to give Gloria a preview of the exciting things that lie ahead.

> *Looks like it's your turn, Steve. Please copy and send the itinerary page (attached) along with this fax that shows all our travel plans starting next week. Thanks! The Internet server is down again today, so I can't get to the email at all. Mark just told me that tomorrow there's supposed to be a big-time bus strike, so I may or may not come to school tomorrow. God, I hope there isn't a strike on Sunday!!*

This was actually the third version of the itinerary I had drafted weeks earlier. When all was said and done, we would wind up doing most, but not all, of the trips listed.

• • •

Besides all the faxes, e-mails, and phone calls to keep in touch, on several occasions I had sent a small gift or card back home to let Gloria know she was in my thoughts. Like candy from the pasticceria. Embroidered handkerchiefs and lace doilies that I bought at the open market in Piazza

Itinerary-B
PETER & GLORIA

Rev

DATE	DEP	ARR	DESTINATION	TO DO
11-23 Th	9a	2p	Padua/Venice Leon Bianco Hotel	The Canals; Piazza San Marco; Murano? Harry's Bar; Padua stuff; shopping
11-25 Sat	8a	2p	Santa Margherita Hotel Laurin	Portwalk area; Portofino; Cinque Terra; shopping; La Spezia?
11-27 M	10a	1p	Torino	
12-1 F	9a	3p	Athens Hotel:	Peter & Franca; The Parthenon; other temples/museums; shopping
12-3 Sun	4p	8p	Torino	
12-4 M	9a 3p	11a 5p	St. Vincent Torino	Daytrip to the mountains & return
12-7 Th	7a	11a	Pisa/Florence Hotel Hermitage	Leaning Tower; Uffizi; shopping
12-8 F **	11a	5p	Sorrento Hotel Bristol	The ocean; Isle of Capri; Amalfi; Cafe Royale; shopping
12-10 Sun	9a 11a	1p 3p	Rome Grand Hotel Flora	St. Peter's; Sistine Chapel; Roman Forum; Coliseum; St. John Lateran; San Stefano Catacombs? Caracalla Baths? Pantheon? Spanish Steps; Trevi Fountain; Piazza Navona; Buggy ride at night; Derby Restaurant; shopping; Note: Open market at Porta Portese only on Sundays
12-13 W	7a	9a	Florence Hotel Brunelleschi	The Uffizi; Accademia Gallery; Pitti Palace; Ponte Vecchio; Santo Spirito Church; San Gimignano; Sienna? shopping
12-15 F	7a 11:p 5:30p	10p 3:30p 7p	Milan San Bernardino Locarno Hotel Muralto (LA)	The Duomo (check luggage) Ski lodge (train to Bellinzona, then bus) The lake; Madonna del Sasso church; Castillo Vittelo; Ascona? casino; shopping
12-16 Sat	4p	8p	Malpensa Airport Hotel Villa Malpensa (LA)	(Train to Milan Centrale, via Bellinzona, then bus to Malpensa Airport, then cab to hotel)
12-17 Sun	12:25	7:25	Cincinnati	

** Festiva LA=Guarantee for late arrival

Guala. Gold earrings and a gold cross that I found in a jewelry store in the neighborhood. Italian greeting cards and postcards, a cute one that simply said, "*Ho bisogno di te*" ("I need you" or, literally, "I have need of you."). And more candy.

Before leaving Dayton, I had had the foresight to think ahead toward two of our monthly anniversaries for which we would be apart—September 19th and October 19th. So, in August, right before I left, I ordered some flowers to be delivered on those dates and also stashed a couple of small personal gift items in secret places around the house. These could later be "discovered" by Gloria with a little prompting by her *marito* (husband) from afar. Which is exactly how it worked out, much to her (and my) delight.

One gift, for example, I hid in the back of a closet with notes leading her from one place to another, to another, and finally to the closet. To get the search started I sent clues in a fax from Italy (like the one below) directing her to the first hidden note.

There were other emotional moments, too, times when I asked myself what was I doing in Italy anyway. Like the day I received a fax from Geno with distressing news about my grandson, Kyle, then five years old. Kyle was born with Fragile X Syndrome, a genetic condition that causes mental retardation and mental illness. As Kyle was growing older, he was becoming increasingly difficult to control. He would turn angry for no apparent reason, banging his head against the TV, walls, and doors. Sometimes he would turn violent against his parents and his older sister.

Writing to me in Italy about turning Kyle over to a foster home was exceedingly painful for Geno. I recall reading his words while standing outside the school that day. It really tore me up inside. And made me feel quite alone and helpless.

> TO: GLORIA J. CARUSONE, UAW Office
> ☹☹☹☹☹☹☹☹ without you ☹☹☹☹☹☹☹☹
> ☺☺☺☺☺☺☺☺ waiting for you ☺☺☺☺☺☺☺☺
> ☺☺☺☺☺☺☺☺ with you ☺☺☺☺☺☺☺☺
>
> Happy Anniversary, Darling!!!!!!!!!!!
>
> Love, Peter
>
> 📫📫📫📫📫📫📫📫📫📫📫📫📫📫📫📫📫📫📫📫📫📫
> 📫
>
> I have a gift for you,
> My love so true!
> If you'll just check it out when you get home
> You'll know how close I feel to you,
> No matter how far my travels make me roam.
>
> To be in your arms would be like in heaven,
> So see what's there for you on page 187
> In a book called "THE STORY," *
> My darling Glory!
>
> Pluck what's there
> But first,
> Read the verse;
> And you'll know how
> deeply for you I care
>
> I love you!
>
> *Clue: To find the book, look on the top shelf of the bookcase at the top of the stairs, the one just outside our bedroom door. Good luck!

Dad,

    How are things in Italy by now? Are you getting adjusted to your new surroundings yet? I'm sure you're having an exciting time. I got your three e-mail messages yesterday, and passed the one on to Gloria. It sounds like you're not having much luck with your laptop as far as the modem is concerned. You mentioned that you were using someone else's computer. Gloria mentioned that you would like me to get your fax modem software working on your PC at home. I'll try to get to that soon.

I had my first test in Statics and Dynamics on Wednesday, the day after I got back in town. I got a 78, which I was pleased with since I went into it without studying at all.

Things at home aren't going very well right now. Kyle has been getting progressively worse with his behavior. Cindy and I have come to the conclusion that he needs to be in a different environment. I know he loves us and wants to be with us, but he can't handle the surroundings he is in. He seems so much happier when he is in school & daycare. And we can't keep going on believing that everything will be all right. We have been looking around for a place for him & nobody seemed to want to help us.

We did come across a place up north that has an opening and we are going there on Monday to look at it. It is privately funded. They have a 1500-acre complex. Their goal is to teach the kids to better deal with themselves in society.

I hope you understand what we are doing. We are not doing this because he is an inconvenience. We just can't handle it anymore. We love him very much and feel so guilty for doing this. We really need everybody's support with this. It's something that we can try. If things don't work out we can always bring him back home.

Dad, why do things turn out like this? I feel like if this does happen that I'm losing my son, and that he will think we don't love him or want to be with him. It's not his fault, he can't help the way he is. I feel like I'm punishing him for something he has no control over. I am going to get back to work now. I'll talk to you soon.

Love always,
Geno

I spent much of the afternoon that day in the computer lab composing a response to Geno's fax. At first, I didn't know what to say. Then I just started writing as though Geno were sitting across the table from me. I didn't know how much my words of consolation would help but hoped that somehow I could make a difference. At any rate, I was grateful, as always, for having been blessed with kids who are open with me about their problems, and not shy to ask for advice, or use me as a sounding board.

Hi, Geno,
Just received your fax from Saturday. Hey, you did real well for not studying on that test! Maybe you should try that technique on all the tests...you will do better than you did last year when you were studying—haha!
Sounds like you and Cindy are really struggling with the situation about Kyle. Geno, we all empathize and we think we understand how hard it must be for you, but we don't really know because we are not in your shoes. Sure, we miss not seeing Kyle when he is not at the family functions. We love him and enjoy him, especially when he is on his good behavior which seems like most of the time that he spends with us. But that is not his normal environment. I know he is often a different person when he is out than when he is at home. He is growing older and more aggressive and more difficult to control. Maybe this is what he needs—if he is happier in school and daycare, if they can teach him what he needs to learn in order to grow up and function in society.

We can pledge you our support, Geno, in your decision to find a place for him but that will probably not reduce the pain you will feel when it happens. Here is what I think. It is always very difficult for us (as parents) to let go. Sometimes it is easier, perhaps, as when they go off to college for awhile or get married and remain in the area. Sometimes it is not so easy, as in divorce cases, or someone who elopes at an early age, or gets pregnant out of wedlock. But it is never easy for parents to let go of their children, even though they (the children) have their own life to lead.

Ask yourself, what is in Kyle's best interest? Maybe you are just having to let go of him, and do what's best for him, a little sooner than most parents, you know? I guess it reminds me of a mother bird pushing her baby out of the nest even though the baby does not know how to fly. I think if this is what he needs and if you can keep in touch as an important part of his life, then you have done all you could for his benefit, not yours.

Why things turn out like this? Well, they say God has a reason for everything, and that he often works in mysterious ways. I don't know.

Let me know how this place looks. I need to get a copy of USA Today *to find out when the Reds start play in the World Series! Take care, son.*

Love,
Dad

Just before I walked into Jera's office and retrieved Geno's fax along with my mail, I had been participating in an Italian language class, engaged in a touching dialogue with the instructor. She called on me to do the exercise that asked where I would like to be at that moment. I said *nella stati uniti* (in the United States). She asked why? I said to be with *la mia molgie* (my wife). She asked what present I would bring to my wife. I said *un bacio* (a kiss). The students in the class were smiling and exchanging glances. The whole discussion was in Italian, so it was a touching and sentimental moment. As you can imagine, by the end of the day I felt like I was on an emotional roller coaster.

. . .

> *Well, today is Gloria's last day at work for awhile; she'll be home Friday doing last minute things. Saturday she'll be traveling all day and, of course, on Sunday I'll be meeting and greeting her at the Milan airport (at about 9 A.M.). I have to get up at 4:30 Sun. morning (Oh, no!) to catch a 6:00 A.M. tram to go downtown to the bus terminal, then take the 7:15 bus to the airport. I have to get some snacks in just in case we're hungry when we get to the apartment—(remember, stores are all closed on Sunday). But the pizzerias are open on Sunday night (they close on Monday) so I can take her to Noe's, my favorite local hangout for good pasta and pizza.*

The trip to the airport on Sunday went pretty much according to plan, though I don't think anyone back home could have comprehended what I would have to go through to get to the airport on that cold dark November Sunday morning. "In Italy," someone had said, "nothing is easy!"

I awoke at the appointed hour with the help of my trusty travel alarm. It was dark and cold outside, as it was supposed to be. The streets were deserted. I walked nearly a mile to the place where I needed to catch the tram. The tram was a few minutes late but got me downtown with time to spare. After a brisk walk to the intercity bus terminal, a walk of another half-mile or so, I was ready for some hot coffee.

Inside, the aroma coming from the bar was wonderful. Trays of briosche were being served hot, right out of the oven, and out of this world! The cappuccino was fresh and steaming hot. Now, there is nothing like a freshly baked briosche and a steaming cup of cappuccino on a cold dark morning to make one feel warm and fuzzy inside. In fact, believe it or not, this was one of the highlights of the trip!

There were quite a few people waiting for buses. As the time got close, I kept running outside to check the bay from which the airport bus was supposed to depart because they have been known to switch bays on you when you are not looking. Sure enough, I soon discovered that the bus I was waiting for had pulled into a different bay than the one I was told it would! When I felt 99 percent certain that I had identified the correct bus, I boarded and waited patiently for departure. Daylight was beginning to break as we pulled out of the parking lot and headed for Malpensa airport.

Now, the distance from Torino to Malpensa is about an hour and a half by bus (quite a bit less by car as we would discover on the return trip to Torino). The bus was tooling along at a decent speed. Then a man walked to the front of the bus, leaned over, and said something to the driver. I could hear their voices but could not understand what they were saying. They were in a heated argument about something. The bus driver was quite animated and vocal, clearly agitated.

The passenger meekly backed away and sat down immediately behind the driver, as if waiting for further instructions. He reminded me of a schoolboy made to sit in a corner. After another five or ten minutes the bus suddenly pulled off to the side of the road and came to a full stop. The doors swung wide open. The man who had come to the front of the bus jumped off and ran about 100 feet down the road. He stood with his back to the bus, taking a leak by the side of the road! I couldn't believe my eyes! A few minutes later, the man hurries back onto the bus, bowing in deference to the driver. *"Grazie. Grazie,"* while the driver is still throwing out some choice words and gestures reaffirming his disapproval.

• • •

Michael, an Italian, had occupied a seat next to Gloria on the plane during her eight-hour flight from New York. He was returning home from a computer show in Las Vegas, carrying with him a sizable carton of software. Gloria said he was very nice and even offered to give us a ride to Torino in his car. I said "Great, this will be something different."

His English was good enough for us to carry on a simple conversation, but not much more. Once we got on the *autostrada*, I noticed the speedometer was hanging pretty much at or above 150 kph, that is, 100 miles per hour.

Michael said he was not married but rather lived with a girlfriend, which seems to be a popular kind of arrangement in the North (no wonder the divorce rate is so low!). When we arrived in Torino, Michael stopped at a *pasticceria* while Gloria and I waited in the car. When he returned, he brought with him two nicely wrapped packages, one for us as it turned out, the other for his girlfriend. Inside were more delicious pastries for us to enjoy! A nice gesture of welcome from a native Italian.

• • •

I almost named this chapter "Gloria Arrived and the Earth Shook!!" A few nights after Gloria's arrival, I woke up suddenly in the middle of the night, sat up in bed, and watched the walls and the wardrobe shake. I thought maybe the scene was part of a dream. Then, I thought… *what are the people in the apartment next door doing, trying to break down the wall?!*

The next morning, we learned from the news that the shaking had been an earthquake, centered some distance from Torino. Italy is a high-risk area for earthquakes. Three thousand of its 8,000 towns are in constant threat of being subjected to earthquake, which affects approximately 10 million homes, or 40 percent of the national total. The earthquake had happened at 3 A.M., and registered "4" or "5" on the Richter scale! There did not seem to be any serious injuries or damage in the local area.

. . .

During Gloria's visit, I tried to help her acclimate to her new surroundings. We toured the neighborhood and I showed her my favorite shops and restaurants. I introduced her to the candy store ladies, and the family that owns and operates Noe's Pizzeria. She accompanied me to school several times and even sat in on my classes once, which happened to be two days after her arrival. I recall this vividly because she was still so exhausted from jetlag that she actually started dozing right in the middle of my lecture!

The first item on our itinerary was a trip to Venice and we were raring to go! The five-day excursion would allow us to enjoy Padua and Venice for two nights, then spend another two nights in Santa Margherita while visiting Cinque Terra and Portofino on the Italian Riviera. This turned out to be another time when we would have to abide by the admonition, "In Italy, you have to be flexible."

We had been warned that this was probably the worst time of the year to go to Venice due to the fog, rain, and cold temperatures, but that places further south would have milder weather. Of course, we didn't have much choice and were grateful that at least we wouldn't have to fight the crowds of the high season.

When we arrived in Venice it was about 3:00 P.M. on a Thursday that just happened to be Thanksgiving Day in the States (not a holiday in Italy). Remember, this is a time of the day when all restaurants are closed.

As we would soon discover, Venice is famous for bad—and pricey—restaurants. Of course, when you have the uniqueness of a canal city without cars, the splendor of San Marco Square, and the beauty of the blown glass produced right there on nearby Murano, I guess you don't have to have good restaurants or reasonable prices. One travel guide advises "all is not lost, if one has the Michelin Red Guide and a billfold about 20% thicker than would be necessary on the mainland."

Our first goal when we arrived was to find our way to Piazza San Marco, shopping along the way, of course. You have to remember that in Venice there are only two ways to get around. One is by boat. The gondolas commonly identified with Venice and the city's romantic image are outrageously expensive. If you are lucky you will get maybe a half-an-hour or 45 minuti for close to $100! A more rational alternative is to take the vaporetto, or water taxi. A vaporetto is a ferry with routes and stops just like an autobus.

The second way to get around in Venice is *a piedi* (on foot). Well, we walked. And walked. And walked! We stopped and shopped and enjoyed the scenery, as frigid as it was (about 20 degrees Fahrenheit, but even colder due to all the water and marble), and we kept looking for San Marco Square. Signs everywhere pointed us this way, then that way. After awhile it became a joke. One sign for San Marco actually showed arrows pointing in two opposite directions. We wondered if there really was a *Piazza San Marco*!

Once we found it, we were truly impressed. Such a huge and wonderful space! Surrounded by palaces, churches and other buildings of ornate Byzantine and

Gothic architecture, it is a magnificent space. A natural hangout for pigeons and people, a great place to walk and enjoy the surroundings, not the least of which are rows of shops and sidewalk cafes.

We stopped at an elegant café by the name of Florian's to enjoy a fancy pastry and something hot to drink. Florian's has been around since 1720. It was a favorite hangout for Venetians during the Austrian occupation. Elegant. Popular. And pricey. But the pastries are awesome!

We also stopped at the famous Harry's Bar where we ordered a Bellini, which was invented there and is associated with a guy named Hemingway, the bar's most famous customer. Happily (for the owner), many of the famous tycoons and countesses who used to frequent Harry's Bar also liked the Bellini and so it became even more famous. And so did the bar!

What is a Bellini, you say? It is an Italian twist on the classic Mimosa, substituting peach juice for orange juice. To make one, you need two ingredients: (1) peach juice or canned peach nectar, topped off with (2) chilled champagne, preferably an Italian sparkling wine. Use half of each. Fresh peach juice is probably the best, of course, but you can also substitute a peach liqueur. If you do, use only a small amount, not half. Since the flavor of the peach juice becomes predominant, it is not necessary to use an expensive champagne—a cheap one will work just fine. Another *caveat*—never, but never, prepare Bellinis ahead of time.

Today, Harry's Bar has become a very popular tourist attraction, despite its not-so-popular prices. But, there is some disagreement as to whether Hemingway actually liked drinking Bellinis or not. Here is what a travel guide on the Internet has to say about it:

> *Sit at the bar and drink a Bellini, invented here, and then think about the fact that Hemingway probably sat in exactly the same spot and drank exactly the same drink. Then remind yourself that Hemingway was a real man who wouldn't have been caught dead drinking a sissy drink like peach juice and sparkling wine.*

When Gloria and I walked into Harry's, we thought it might be a good place to eat. You know, splurge a little. We quickly realized we were wrong. The place was packed and we could see that we would be lucky to find someone to make us a drink and take our money, assuming we had enough money to pay the bill!

Eventually, we were able to find a table, get the attention of a waiter, and place an order for two of the world-famous Bellinis. The verdict was "Good, but not great." If it were a term paper I would give it a B+. And to make matters worse, they didn't even offer any snacks, like the nuts and tidbits that commonly sit on the tables of most Italian bars. It's a good thing we decided not to eat there!

After returning to the States, a new Italian restaurant named Bravo's opened near our residence in Dayton. The first time Gloria and I went there, we sat at the bar and ordered a Bellini. The bar people said they never heard of a Bellini. Or Harry's Bar for that matter!

. . .

From Venice, we took the train to Santa Margherita and checked into Hotel Laurin, a Best Western. We walked around and enjoyed the beauty of the harbor, shopped, and enjoyed Saturday evening dinner *al fresco*. As luck would have it, it started to rain before we could make it back to the hotel, and did so on into the night. This severely curtailed our plans as the skies were still pouring *gatti e cani* (cats and dogs) when we awoke the next morning. So, we decided to skip Portofino and Cinque Terra, which would have involved a lot of walking outside, and instead decided "to be flexible."

Pisa, I remembered, was one of the few places where some shops and restaurants are actually open on Sundays. So we caught a southbound train and headed for the city of the leaning tower. We returned to Torino later that night. It was the end of Gloria's first week in Italy.

In retrospect, it was a wonderful week. Given Gloria's arrival on my birthday, it was only fitting that about two weeks later, on December 5th, it was Gloria's turn to celebrate a birthday. *Buon compleanno! Salute!*

Ironically, it was not until a year after our return to Ohio that I learned the true meaning of the word "*Compleanno.*" (I had always thought it a strange-sounding word compared to the sentiments it was intended to express. Perhaps I was looking for something more "Italian," like "*Buon Bortday*"?) Ida, an Italian instructor from whom I was taking a refresher course, explained the word to me. She broke it into two parts, and said <u>compleanno</u> stands for <u>completo</u>-<u>anno</u>, or complete year!

16

ROMA

In 1870 Italian troops entered Rome on the heels of the French garrison withdrawal. The unification of the Kingdom of Italy was complete.

I had the good fortune to be able to visit Rome twice, first by myself and later with Gloria. St. Peter's and the Vatican. The Coliseum. Michelangelo's *Pieta*. The Roman Forum, the Baths of Caracalla, and, of course, the Derby Restaurant...twice. (Sounds like I got stuck in a rut, doesn't it?) There were so many things I enjoyed so much that I was eager to share them with Gloria, and see them a second time.

What fascinated me most about Rome is the realization, and the constant visible reminders, that so many momentous historical events took place right there! I eventually came to see Rome not as just another Italian city, but as a symbol of Italy and the Italian people. A symbol of the days of the great Roman Empire. Of the "one, holy, catholic, and apostolic Church." And, as a symbol of the relationship between the Italian people and the Roman Catholic Church. This relationship I like to characterize as "one foot in and one foot out."

. . .

Rome was the last holdout. It took nine years after Italy became a nation in 1861 for Rome to become a part of it! Ten years after Garibaldi and the Thousand had captured Sicily and the south, Rome was finally taken for the new kingdom. And the capital moved once again, ever further south—from Torino to Florence, and finally to Rome.

As Rome became part of the new Italy, the temporal power of the Church was legally abolished. The Pope did not take kindly to this turn of events. He threatened to excommunicate anyone who voted or otherwise participated in the new Italian state. The only geography remaining in the pope's hands was the Vatican, the church of San Giovanni in Laterano (St. John Lateran), and the summer residence in Castelgandolfo.

When the Italian army marched unhindered into Rome on September 20, 1870, the pope voluntarily sequestered himself in his state. For nearly 60 years thereafter, no pope would emerge from the confines of the Vatican.

At one time "the Papal Lands" spread over large sections of what is now Italy. The Church, often with the aid of a foreign power like France or Spain, controlled vast expanses of land, people and money, especially through the central regions.

The clergy were not inclined to negotiate with an upstart government, and that was the case for many years. In the final analysis, it was Mussolini, of all people, who in 1929 got together with the Pope and concluded some important agreements. They signed the original Concordat and Lateran Treaty which, among other things, officially created the separate and sovereign entity of Vatican City.

Now what is the big deal about all this historical stuff? What does this have to do with Rome and Italy today? Well, I believe that a bit of historical perspective can go a long way. It can be quite useful by creating a context for what one sees.

For example, I grew up with the impression that Italy and Roman Catholicism were inseparable, that all Italians were good Catholics, and that all the Popes were Italian. These facts were not historically accurate, nor are they true today.

At one time divorce and abortion in Italy were unthinkable. By the 1970s, the Italians legalized divorce and abortion and today they are more common than ever, though not nearly as prevalent as in countries like the United States of America.

Visit the Vatican, stand inside the 2,000 year-old Coliseum, or just mosey around the Spanish Square— I believe that the more you know about the history of the place, the better you will understand and enjoy what you are seeing.

A memory from my own history: When I was growing up, my dad, aunts and uncles, and grandparents attended Sunday Mass at St. Francis Seraph Church at Liberty and Vine Streets in Cincinnati. My grandparents and the married aunts and uncles always managed to get to the church in plenty of time and take their seats up front. But my dad, single at the time, and my single uncles usually came in late (probably because they had been out late the night before!). At any rate, rather than look for a seat, they seemed to prefer standing in the back. As though with one foot in and one foot out.

I think that is the kind of relationship Italians have with their Church. One foot in and one foot out. They like having the Pope and the Vatican in their back yard, but don't want the limitations of having to live by his rules.

I picked up similar attitudes, incidentally, about Americans. Italians give the impression they like their connection with America, but they also seem to delight in pointing out Americans' shortcomings. For example, the Italians I met often commented that "Americans are selfish." They also asked, "Why are there so many shootings in America?"

. . .

Rome today is a modern city steeped in the traditions and legends of ancient and not-so-ancient history. Rome is the Eternal City and always has been. All roads lead there... so it is said.

It is also said that Rome is "just another big city." As such, it lacks the intimacy of Florence, the character of Venice, and the sophistication of Milan. It is simply Rome.

Romans have an attitude, a kind of lofty air, but not the snobbishness often associated with the Milanese. Perhaps a touch of showmanship and a dash of braggadocio. Like the staff guy behind the desk at the hotel where we stayed on Via Veneto who wore a cape and was forever swooshing and fluttering all over the place.

. . .

A gentleman by the name of Ettore tells the story of his adult son's experience in Rome, an encounter that demonstrates how easily Italians from one region can spot someone from another part of Italy just by hearing them utter a few words.

Ettore's son, Franco, was raised in Milan until he was 10, when the family moved to the USA. To this day, Franco speaks both Italian and English. Well, there he was, a passenger at the Rome International Airport, waiting to board the bus to take them into the city. He was in a crowd of people, mostly Italians not known for waiting in an orderly line, all eager to board the bus.

Then, along comes this guy who cuts right in front of everybody and starts up the steps to the bus. Well, Ettore's son, in his best Italian, calls out to the man: "Why don't you come down here and wait in line like us?" The man stops and turns toward Franco and yells back: "Eh, stronzo milanese! No lo sapere che io sono il guidatore?"

Translation: "Hey Turd of Milan, don't you know that I am the driver?"

. . .

What impresses me most about Rome are the remarkable contrasts: between sacred and secular, ancient and modern, conservative and avant-garde.

The icons of Christianity are unmistakable. Even so, there are likewise symbols and manifestations of the strictly civil and even pagan faces of both modern and Ancient Rome. On one corner you may see remains of the 2,000-year-old Coliseum where Christians were thrown to the lions for entertainment, and on another, shrines and grottos, reminders of devotion to Jesus, Mary, and the Saints, reminders of Christianity and Catholicism.

Whether you're visiting the Roman Forum, the Coliseum, or touring through various neighborhoods of the city, you cannot avoid the walls and ruins of Ancient Rome. They are all around! When I think of Rome, that's what I see. The ancient ruins and those magnificent 2,000-year-old walls that so often have become integrated with more modern edifices and new land uses. I envision Roman legions marching alongside those remarkable walls. And I picture Roman soldiers and little boys playing a game of bocce ball.

With all the visual cues, it is not too difficult to imagine what life must have been like in the days of the Holy Roman Empire. Those incredible walls and crumbling remains of fortresses are to be found, incidentally, not only in Rome but throughout Italy and other parts of Europe.

. . .

After St. Peter's and Vatican City, the Coliseum, the Roman Forum, and perhaps the Pantheon, what more is there to see in Rome? Well, for me, there were two other attractions I especially enjoyed because they were "off the beaten track," and previously unknown to me.

The first is a huge complex called the Baths of Caracalla. Like a big park, it consists of acres and acres of land. The Ancient Romans went there to relax. It was a spa, and you can still see evidence of where the various pools, rooms, and other features of the complex used to be. In addition to three pools (hot, warm and cold), the *Terme di Caracalla* boasted exercise rooms, libraries and lecture halls. Today, open-air opera is presented there in the summer.

The other interesting place I discovered is a beautiful, often-overlooked church. Some say it is even more beautiful than St. Peter's. This is the church of St. John Lateran, the duomo (cathedral) of Rome, located a couple of subway stops from the Coliseum, and is the Pope's parish in his capacity as bishop of Rome. This church is prominently listed on major tourist maps but I don't know how many visitors actually see it as it is some distance from the other main attractions. There is a lot of history here, including the hosting of various worldwide ecumenical councils and the signing of the Lateran Treaty. The paintings and sculptures inside the church are well worth a visit.

. . .

Roman soldiers used to play the bocce game. When I try to envision it, I can't decide whether they might have played it with rocks, balls, or what!

Some say bocce had its origins in Egypt as far back as 5200 B.C.! If that's true, then bocce is the oldest sport in human history. From Egypt, the game is believed to have spread throughout the Middle East and Asia, and eventually to Greece. The Greeks then introduced it to the Romans, and the Romans, of course, spread the game to the rest of the known world.

Many people still are unfamiliar with the game of bocce ball. The British call it lawn bowling. One source defines it as a game played with wooden balls on a long, narrow court covered with fine gravel. An official court is 60 or 76 feet long and may be sunken 6 inches into the ground, with wood beams around the perimeter, giving it a playing area that resembles a billiards table. The balls used today are ceramic-like and the game can be played almost anywhere, including the beach or the lawn.

In the late 19th century, Italian immigrants brought their game of bocce to the United States, Australia, Argentina, and other countries where it is widely played today. Currently it is undergoing a surge of popularity. Bocce courts are being built as part of retirement communities, senior citizen centers, and public recreation areas, especially in California, but also in places like Pennsylvania, Ohio, Wisconsin, and Canada.

The appeal of the game is not just that it's fun, which it is, but that anyone can play—old, young, strong, or feeble. There is a lot of skill and strategy involved, as my sons and I learned soon after joining the men's bocce league at the Sons of Italy lodge. We lost almost every game the first year, often playing against men in their 70s and 80s!

. . .

He stepped off the curb, ambled without hesitation to the middle of the street, then turned and stopped to face the oncoming car, as if daring it to hit him. We refer to this unknown man who helped us across the street as the "daredevil pedestrian of Vatican City!"

Gloria and I were traveling from the Vatican Museums and Sistine Chapel to St. Peter's Square. We were standing at the curb waiting for a break in the traffic as one car after another came barreling down the hill. I said something to Gloria, shouting to be heard above the noise of the traffic, about how Italian drivers apparently lack the courtesy to let pedestrians cross a street. I must have said it loudly enough for the man standing near us to hear me. That's when he stepped off the curb and stopped the traffic. I sure was glad to see the car stop because this man refused to budge!

. . .

We did plenty of walking in Rome. Many of the attractions are spaced far apart, but not far enough to wait for another bus or the metro and, besides, there is much to see along the way. And the exercise is good for you. But the streets are not exactly pedestrian-friendly. In fact the streets of Rome are about the widest you will find in Italy. Sometimes it takes two rotations of the traffic signal to make it across completely from one side to the other.

We walked Via Veneto, a beautiful street that winds up a steep hill, several times. Our hotel was located there, at the top. The nearest metro station was close to a mile away and down at the bottom of the hill. Every day, we passed the U.S. Embassy as police vans and armed guards stood by.

. . .

Another great place to walk, where thousands of Romans and tourists take their nightly stroll (*passeggiata*), is Via Condotti, in the Piazza di Spagna (Spanish Square). The shops on Via Condotti are the most upscale in Rome.

The complex surrounding the famous Scala di Spagna (Spanish Steps) is a real magnet for people of all ages. The area includes an expansive plaza, an impressive historical fountain, an important obelisk, the famous steps, the church at the top of the steps, a building next to the steps where some famous British poets once lived, a nearby popular McDonald's restaurant and, of course, Via Condotti.

The plaza at the bottom of the Steps teems with people, street vendors, and horse-drawn buggies for hire. "The Steps" (all 137 of them), which lead from the Piazza up to the Church of Trinita dei Monti, were built in 1725.

. . .

Why is everyone so interested to know what McDonalds in other countries are like? I mean, a McD is a McD, right?! Wrong.

Probably the most popular McDonalds in all of Italy is the one near the Spanish Steps. It has great location, not only for young locals and nostalgic tourists, but for anyone who may be hungry at times of the day when the Italian restaurants are all closed! (For the record, I cannot imagine wanting to go to a McDonald's in Italy except for cultural curiosity, which is why I went there.)

This particular McDonald's is huge. When you enter from Via Due Macelli, the first thing you encounter is a lobby with a gelateria serving ice cream. A little further a hallway leads to the main part of the restaurant. The dining room is spacious, perhaps three times the size of your typical McD's in the States.

The main menu looks similar to any McDonald's in the USA. However, once you get beyond hamburgers and fries, some things are quite different. The menu offers beer and a salad bar that features various Italian appetizers and side dishes like peas, beans, marinated peppers, and even pastas.

. . .

We disagreed on the price. We just wanted a simple, short, and romantic ride from Piazza di Spagna to nearby Trevi Fountain, and back.

It was a beautiful December Sunday evening and Piazza di Spagna was packed. People sat around Bernini's fountain. Crowds gathered near the steps, which were still closed for remodeling. People walking... always walking. It was a crush of humanity. Maybe a good time for the horse and buggy ride we'd been wanting to do? But how would the carriage move through this sea of humanity without knocking down some people?

But despite our worry, we found a buggy and driver. An elderly Italian with leathery skin and a serious demeanor, the driver wanted 200,000 lire to take us to Trevi Fountain and some other nearby places. I said we only wanted to do Trevi, not the other places. He then offered us a 100,000 lire deal, insisting "It costs a lot to feed and care for *il cavallo* (the horse)!"

Gloria and I were not looking for the deluxe tour at the time nor were we looking to buy his horse!

"*Troppo caro* (too dear)," I said. It's a good phrase to remember when you go shopping (and sometimes it actually works to bring down the price). I'm sure he wanted me to feel sorry for him, or for the horse, but I stuck to my guns and told him I still thought that it was troppo caro. Then he brought the price down to 50,000 lire.

"*Va bene!*" (Deal!).

All the worry about the sea of humanity standing in the way of our buggy ride was for naught. Once we agreed on a price (negotiating really was the fun part) and were securely seated, the driver cracked his whip, yelled to the horse, and like the Red Sea parting for Moses, the people in front of us quickly moved to one side or the other.

About an hour later, after the driver had returned us to the Spanish Steps, he turned to me for payment. I politely gave him the 50,000 lire we had agreed on and told him, "*Per il cavallo* (for the horse)."

Then, with a smile on my face, I handed him a tip of another 10,000 lire and said, "*Per te* (for you)." I couldn't tell whether or not he appreciated the humor.

17

MAGNA ITALIA

The Roman Empire, at its height, included about a fourth of Europe, much of the Middle East, and the entire coastal area of North Africa. More than 1,500 years after its demise, the Roman Empire still influences our lives today.
—World Book Encyclopedia

How does Italy relate to the countries around it? Are the peoples of the various European countries becoming more alike or different? Is a new unified culture emerging in the region?

It is increasingly important to view Italy, not as some isolated enclave but, in a broader sense, as an integral part of the European Union, NATO, and the Western World of freedom-loving nations. Although it is the local culture that is the most interesting about life on the Italian peninsula, today and yesterday, it is Italy's evolving role in the family of nations that will affect its political and economic standing tomorrow.

I used to think that Italy would be a relatively closed society, a country unto itself, totally separate and different than any other country in the region. After all, the geography is such that the peninsula is substantially removed from mainland Europe.

Yet over the centuries a lot of interchange and integration among the countries and peoples of the region has occurred, not just among the nationalities of Europe but of the whole Mediterranean basin and beyond. So, I should not have been surprised, as I was, to find so many Italian and Roman influences throughout the neighboring countries.

. . .

Magna Italia! The history books talk about Magna Grecia, but what I saw in my limited travels was more a reflection of Magna Roma, or Greater Italy (with all due respect to my Greek friends, Peter "A," George, and Nick).

This chapter is about the travels that took me beyond the boot, however briefly. The extensive network of walls and ruins emanating from Rome. The coming together of previously divided and formerly antagonistic European countries into a cohesive trading and social unit. The marvelous integration of antiquities with modern and contemporary architectural styles.

A good example of this integration can be found in downtown Torino (as well as in Rome, Athens, and other European cities) where Roman walls have become part of more modern edifices. An especially interesting architectural anomaly is a 15th-century castle in downtown Torino called Palazzo Madama, about which I wrote to Gloria and her son, Christopher, the architecture student:

> *I am going to send you a postcard (inside a letter) to forward to Chris. It's a photo of this building downtown called the Palazzo Madama.*

> *The main part of the structure looks like ancient Roman walls and then a facade was added on later. Really weird looking.*

Outside Italy, I spent time in Greece, Switzerland, Germany, and Austria. Much of what I saw in those countries reminded me of the expansive Roman empire depicted in books and movies of a generation gone by. I was taken aback by the similar Roman remnants and evidences of Oriental and North African influences.

The Egyptian connection was especially intriguing. I had never considered a possible link between Italy and Egypt. Then I discovered that Egypt was Italy's breadbasket during the Roman Empire. Throughout Italy today, you see various obelisks and artifacts from Egypt, such as the tall, imposing obelisk near St. John Lateran church in Rome, and the Egyptian museum in Torino, renowned to be the second-largest Egyptian museum in the world!

Egypt was the beneficiary, too, of projects undertaken by Roman troops, such as the clearing of the canals under the emperor Probus in the third century A.D. Not unlike the USA, Rome was truly a world power and acted in sometimes benevolent ways toward its neighbors.

. . .

As my travels took me beyond the land of pasta and pizza, I continued to update my journal and try to convey the highlights to family and friends back home.

> *The trip to Austria-Germany-Switzerland was really interesting. Learned a lot about the influence of the Ancient Romans throughout Europe. The snow in Salzburg was awesome! Saw lots of Mozart and "Sound of Music" stuff there,*

too. The different foods were a nice change of pace.

This one was an easy six-day trip. Easy because it was by train. Easy because I only taught one day that week as the first week of November includes All Saints Day, a Holy Day and secular holiday in Italy.

From Italy I went north by train into the Italian sector of Switzerland, then on to Zurich and Munich (Germany), east into Austria and, finally, south to return to Italy.

One of the interesting, and potentially embarrassing, aspects of the trip was the fact that I had a traveling companion. Her name was Amanda and she was one of the American students. I refer to this situation in a fax to my daughter, Nancy, who had raised the question after learning from Gloria that her dad would be traveling alone with another woman.

Nancy, What do you mean, "traveling alone with another woman?" hahaha. She is not a woman, she's a 20-year-old Iowa farm girl.

The way it happened is that six of us were planning a trip to Barcelona (one male and four female students plus me). That was perfect because we were going to take the overnight train which has sleeper units for six persons, thus, not to worry about strangers taking our stuff.

Well, after four people backed out, for various reasons, that left Amanda and me, still wanting to go to Barcelona. Then, we discovered the train was all booked up and only runs three times a week (M, W, F nights).

So, the alternative was a trip to Zurich, Munich, and Salzburg. Actually, it was sometimes nice to have a travel companion on the trip, but there also were many times I wished I had been on my own.

When the Barcelona trip fell through, Amanda wanted to do Paris and London instead, but not by herself. Well, as I indicated earlier, I had no craving desire to see France in the first place. To make things worse, there were terrorist bombings and threats of bombings in Paris and London.

To her credit, Amanda said she wasn't eager to go where there were bombings, either, so that was an easy out. That's when she got busy researching the tour books and mapped out the Switzerland-Germany-Austria itinerary. I must admit that she did a really great job!

. . .

In Switzerland, I was delighted to discover a gambling casino right where I was staying in beautiful Locarno. That's when I discovered an interesting variation of play on the slot machine—you cannot win unless you first demonstrate some kind of skill! Sounds amazing but it is true.

I was told there is a Swiss law that prohibits pure games of chance. So on every slot machine there is an extra reel with red dots on it that is constantly spinning, though at a slow speed, and can only be stopped (on a dot) by the timely push of a button.

In order to collect a winning jackpot (say, three bells, or three Aces, or whatever) from the machine, the player must stop this extra reel on a red dot. If he does not, then the jackpot cannot be collected, which is exactly what happened to me on more than one occasion after I got overly excited!

. . .

One thing I learned about the Europeans after returning home is that in another hundred years or so, there may not be any! Peter Drucker, international management guru, writing in the *Beta Gamma Sigma News*, says it better than I could:

> *The burden of carrying people who by today's standards of life and health expectancy are still in their best years of middle-age... is simply so great that in all developed countries the people of working age have stopped having children. ...in fact, in Southern Europe, in Italy, Spain, Greece, and Portugal—the countries with the relatively highest retirement benefits, and earliest retirement ages—-the birthrate is already so low (less than half of what is needed to perpetuate the population) that by the end of the next century there will be no Italians, Spaniards, Greeks, or Portuguese left. Even in the U.S., the birthrate is inadequate to replace the population.*

. . .

Is Italy really an integral part of Europe? Here are three unrelated items that allude to the issue of Italy's role on the Continent. See what you think.

The Treaty of Rome, signed in Rome on March 25, 1957, is where it all started. The agreement established a European Economic Community, called the Common Market. The original membership included Belgium, France, West Germany, Italy, Luxembourg, and the Netherlands. The idea was to remove mutual trade barriers in order to promote the economy of Europe and make it a more viable competitor to the United States. To date, the EC has largely been a success.

Marelli, one of the faculty at the school in Torino, was commenting about the latest growing pains between member states of the European Community. The German Prime Minister had been quoted saying unkind things about Italy and other EC countries that were having problems meeting economic targets. With an absolute serious face, Marelli said that he believed Italy should withdraw from the EC and start a new common market together with the Mediterranean countries of Africa!

John F. Kennedy, in a 1960 presidential debate, made a comment directed to the Russians with reference to the generation of Americans who fought in World War II. He said he wanted to send a message to Khrushchev that "a new generation of Americans, who fought in Europe and Italy and the Pacific..." Haha!! Is Italy not part of Europe, I wondered? Sounds like it's not, although the reference undoubtedly is to the three separate fronts in which the fighting had taken place. I think.

. . .

Wondering if there's enough snow to go skiing? It's now possible to get a direct TV picture of weather conditions in the Dolomites (Northeast Italy) on Canale 5 at 8 A.M. on Thursdays and Fridays. These same pictures are being transmitted to Austria and Germany via satellite.

. . .

A flight to Greece for a weekend getaway. Wow, what a trip! What a life!
Compared with Italy's 60 million people, Greece has 10 million, and nearly half of them are living on top of each

other in the city of Athens. Talk about congestion. It took us more than two hours in a private vehicle to get to our hotel from the airport.

If there is any city that needed a metro (subway system), it is Athens. They were in the process of building one when I was there but it was only partially completed, and progress was very slow. It took several years more before it was finally finished!

> We had a great time in Greece this past weekend, visiting our friends from Wright State, Peter and Franca in Athens.
>
> Peter taught at Wright State for five years and was Associate Dean there. His wife, Franca, is an Italian, actually a Siciliana. They used to live in the neighborhood in Dayton...and they remember Nancy as their babysitter and Steve as playing on the soccer team that Peter coached in those days.
>
> Well, they treated us like royalty. Peter is now an executive of a major company. From the minute we arrived, we were chauffeured around and had a private tour guide to the Acropolis (Parthenon) and the National Archeological Museum, and he would not let us pay a cent not even for our hotel, or lunch!
>
> On Saturday night, they put us up at their newly built cottage on their farm in Peter's hometown, about two hours from Athens, on a mountain overlooking the valley and the ocean. It was great! He also showed us the properties where he and Franca are building houses for their three daughters, which combined include orchards of 5,000 orange trees!! I told them we have two sons (Tom & Tony) who would be perfect for his daughters! But, Franca said "Forget it," because

she does not want her daughters to move away to the U.S.

I thought it was such a neat idea, the part about including orange groves that will someday make the daughters' properties self-financing. I wondered if this was a Greek thing, to take care of the offspring in that manner, assuming you can afford it, of course?

. . .

When I bought the airline tickets for the trip to Greece, I discovered that women in Italy apparently keep their maiden names, at least for official purposes, like on passports and other official *documenti*.

When Monica, the travel agent, asked what my wife's name was before we were married, I did not fully comprehend the significance of her question. Nor did I have a clue that it would cause problems down the road due to the fact that the name she was putting on Gloria's airline ticket would turn out to be different than the name on Gloria's passport!

Of course, Monica did not know that Gloria's name "before we were married" was not even her maiden name, but rather her former married name. Nor did she seem to realize that in the States the norm is for women to change their name to their husband's name on all official documents. So, guess what happened when I picked up the airline tickets a few days later? The ticket was wrong and had to be returned because at the airport they will compare your ticket with your passport, and the two had better have the same name!

. . .

In Greece, people are afraid to build on their own property, or to tear down and rebuild, or just to dig, because of the threat of *eminent domain*. They are fearful that they might unearth some remnants of ancient ruins (which are all around the place) and the government will come in and take the property. I think the ruins automatically become public property. I wonder if this might be the case in Italy, too.

• • •

Greeks are proud of their Mediterranean heritage. My friend, Peter, was going on about the healthfulness of olive oil and other key ingredients of the Mediterranean diet. All wholesome, natural foods, including fresh eggs, fruit, and dairy products.

• • •

Just as Italians and Greeks don't like to wait in line, queues are unfamiliar in China, too. An observer on her recent trip there said that queues are unknown, although a Shanghai bank has just introduced the idea. Bank and postal workers may have five or six people crowding their counters, pushing papers and money at them, demanding help. Westerners who wait patiently for a turn will be left standing alone at the end.

Indeed, the Westerner is likely to be ignored as Chinese horn in at the cash register or counter. Maybe a sign that Italian culture has finally penetrated the Orient? The British would be truly bewildered!

• • •

It was George Mikes, a Hungarian-born British author, most famous for his commentaries on various countries, who said: *An Englishman, even if he is alone, forms an orderly queue of one.*

18

MEATBALLS, MISCHIEF & MISCELLANY

Where do meatballs comes from, Italy or America? A student in the Italy class I taught after my return said a friend of hers went to Italy and reported that there were three things she wanted to eat while there but could not find: (1) thick crust pizza, (2) spaghetti with meatballs and, of course, (3) minestrone.

For years I had heard that meatballs did not originate in Italy, but that it was an American (or Italian-American) invention. I accepted this as fact, because I had heard it so many times from different people. I recall thinking about this when I saw the movie *Big Night* and the hilarious scene in which the heathen American couple insists on spaghetti and meatballs, of all things, to supplement their risotto!

So, I began looking for information about the origin of meatballs. I spent days searching for meatball revelations on the Net, even emailed someone in the Parrino family after discovering a "Grandma Parrino" website that contained a recipe for meatballs. They were no help. Don't get me wrong, they are nice people but all they could say is that they did not know whether "Grandma's meatballs" originally came from Italy.

More recently, my nephew Brian spent a few weeks with a family in the southeast part of Italy, near Bari, and told me that, indeed, they did serve meatballs as part of the dinner! Also, several other people I've talked with now claim that meatballs *did* come from the Old Country!

So, what is the truth? Did meatballs come from *Italia* or not? And if they did, why has it been such a well-kept secret? I was determined to get to the bottom of the issue.

...

More on the subject of... *meatballs*. I looked it up in an English-Italian dictionary. Aha, there it is. There is a word for meatballs, so maybe meatball is Italian after all?!

The word for meatball is polpetta di carne. The word carne means meat, but polpetta is not listed in the dictionary by itself.

The next word after meatball in the book is meatloaf. Okay, so what is the Italian word for meatloaf? I got a clue for you, it is NOT a word, it's a sentence!

The translation for meatloaf is polpettone cotto al forno e servito a fette.

Now isn't that a mouthful! Here, let's break it down, word for word, and see what it really says. Look at the words: polpetta (for meatball) and polpettone (for meatloaf). Very similar but the ending is different. Anytime a word ends in tone (I have a feeling that my son, Tony, is going to like this part!), that means that whatever it is, it is a BIG one (opposite of words ending in tina, which means small)!

Therefore, a polpetTONE is a BIG polpetta. I still could not find a direct translation for polpetta, thus, I really don't know the exact meaning. Lorenzo says it is "a big stuff of meal."

Also, it may be instructive to note that *petto* is the word for bosom, and *reggipetto* is the word for bra! Now we are getting somewhere! Maybe a meatball is like a bosom but without the bra?

So meatloaf is a BIG MEATBALL and it is *cotto al forno*, which means it is "cooked in the oven," or baked. (Why don't they just say "baked?!") Also, it is *servito a fette*, which is served sliced. There you have it!

Meatloaf is a big meatball, baked and sliced.

Now I am thinking that if they have to go through this much trouble just to say the word meatball or meatloaf, chances are pretty good that these are not dishes native to Italy, right?

My uncle Armand, however, the good-looking one who was in the U.S. Navy in World War II and has a tendency to talk loudly, full of emotion, strongly disagrees. Last summer when some of us gathered at his house in Girard, Ohio, the conversation about Italian food turned into a heated argument about—of all things—meatballs!

Uncle Armand pointed out that Grandma Mathilde (his mother, my grandmother) used to make meatballs at least once or twice every week ever since anyone could remember. And then I think he made a good point.

"Mom," Uncle Armand insisted, "would never have made those meatballs unless she brought the recipe from Italy." He was yelling pretty loudly by now to make his point so I think he had fairly strong convictions about this!

I recall vividly that my grandmother, who passed away in the 1950s, spoke little English, stayed almost entirely in the house except for family outings, going to church, and visiting relatives, and was not one to readily adapt to American customs, rituals, or food. She likely would not have picked up a recipe for meatballs from Good Housekeeping or Betty Crocker!

• • •

Mischievous Grandpas. "Tella da sister you wanna be da devil!" The man who spoke those words to me did so over 50 years ago and yet I remember hearing them like it was yesterday! I was in first or second grade, walking home from school when he stepped out and greeted me in front of his little clothing shop on Main Street, as he had done on other occasions. I told him about the upcoming school play, and that I would be in it.

That's when, in his best broken English, he said, "Tella da sister you wanna be da devil." I tried to ignore the comment, which I somehow recognized as his way of teasing, but he repeated the directive and was obviously quite amused by it.

His name was Nino Mato (not sure about the spelling). I always identified him with grandpa because he was about the same age, same short and stocky stature, and had pretty much the same accent as grandpa. They were friends, or maybe even related in some way, I don't know.

All the history has been lost. But, I know they both had that same lovingly playful and mischievous air about them.

• • •

Whenever someone asked me if I learned any Italian growing up, I always remembered the cusswords best! Words I learned mainly from Grandpa. Italian grandpas are like that—they're devilish and mischievous! Both my grandpas were, both Grandpa Pietro and Grandpa Stefano.

They were playful and not lacking in expressiveness. They often spoke loud and with sweeping gestures, like being on center stage, teaching me bad words in Italian but never explaining what they meant in English.

I think it is a Latin thing, not just Italian. To some, it sounds terrible that your grandpa would teach you dirty words! For me it was good-natured teasing and bonding. It was assurance of love and a recognition of my emerging role in the familia. It was like letting you in on some of the family secrets. Since the words were in a different language, somehow they didn't sound gross (as they would in English)!

Grandpa Pietro often used the word *vafanculo* (the "F" word), or variations of it. For example, I remember how he used to play "pee pah poom" with me. First, he would take his index finger and touch my stomach, saying "pee!" Then, move his finger up to my chest and with my eyes closely following his finger, he'd say "pah." Finally, in a crescendo as his hand moved up to brush against my mouth and nose with a resounding "POOM!" Then, he would follow the "PEE, PAH, POOM" with an expletive that sounded like "in culo padre," which was not a very flattering thing to say about my dad (his son). The literal translation would be "in your father's butt," or maybe he was simply saying "your father's butt," sort of like the expression "your father's mustache," I don't know.

We would laugh, of course, as if we had just done something naughty together, and at my dad's expense. I recently asked my dad why grandpa would say such a bad thing about him. He just smiled and looked a little puzzled himself.

. . .

Unbelievable! Here I sit, not yet finished writing about my first trip to Italy and already Gloria and I are contemplating a second trip! This time we think we will want to drive a rental car for part of the three weeks we are planning to be there. I say this with some trepidation, of course, knowing full well what I have observed and what I have heard from others about Italian driving. What I am really looking forward to is riding the trains again.

"How they drive in Italy" is a hot topic with Americans. I have noticed that it seems to be the topic people are most curious about, after the food, of course. Here are the kind of questions I have had to address:

Q: **Do they drive on the wrong side of the road?**
A: No, Italians drive on the right side of the road, most of the time.

Q: **Are the traffic signals different than here in the States?**
A: The yellow light stays on longer, and drivers commonly run red lights.

Q: **Are there speed traps?**
A: I am sure there are but I never saw one. I never saw a radar trap, nor did I ever see the police issue a traffic citation to anyone for anything!

Q: **What is the speed limit in Italy?**
A: The official speed limit on the autostrada and other highways ranges from 90 to 130 km/h (55-80 mph), with 50 km/h (30-35 mph) in town. But everybody drives much faster! You often have to get out of their way, keeping in mind that different lanes on the autostrada can have different speed limits. Not a bad idea!

Q: **Why do you prefer riding the trains?**
A: I enjoyed both trains and buses. As Rick Steves points out in one of his books, public transportation

is one of the bargains in Italy and offers other benefits besides:

Trains and buses are inexpensive and good. City-to-city travel is faster, easier, and cheaper by train than by car. Trains give you the convenience and economy of doing long stretches overnight. By train, I arrive relaxed and well-rested—-not so by car.

Q: **Are there many trains to choose from on a given day? And where do you find the schedules?**
A: You can now download train schedules from the Internet, for any given date. Of course, I'm sure they are subject to change. And, you always have to be sure to check the arrival and departure times posted at the terminal because even the track number assigned to a train coming into the station can be changed at the last minute.

Q: **Aren't these schedules difficult to decipher?**
A: The *time* component is pretty easy to follow. But you can get into trouble on some of the other items of information. For example, does the train have a full dining car or simply a snack bar? Does it run only on workdays, or on weekends and holidays as well? (One time I misread one of the symbols and showed up at 6:00 A.M. on a Sunday morning to catch a train that only operated on workdays!)

Q: **Are there special trains you should look for, or ones to avoid?**
A: Yes, the IC (Intercity) trains and the Pendolino (Italy's Bullet train) are the fastest and most modern. But you pay more to ride them, too (it's called a supplement). There is a train called the *accelerato* which sounds like it is going to be a fast

train because the word looks so similar to the word accelerate. But, then you find out it is just the opposite. The *accelerato* makes stops at almost every little town, so that it is forever accelerating! See?!

. . .

Mark is still having difficulty understanding my attitude about the food! He says he hopes my next trip will give me "a more positive experience." I think he just wants to hear me say that the food is wonderful. He doesn't know that much of the time I am just pulling his chain.

Now this is what I was talking about earlier. Believe me, the food in Italia is great! It is much better than what most of us Americans cram down our throats everyday. But, it is not always fantastic, in my opinion, unlike many who report back that "Oh, the food was wonderful!" And it is not always to the liking of the American palate, or even an Italian-American one like mine.

For example, Mark took issue with the fact that I said I never saw *scamorza* cheese there. He says they sell it in the marketplace but not in restaurants, and that it's everywhere. Well, I never saw it! Not once! Nulla! Niente!! Capisce?

Furthermore, he acted like I was wrong when I said more than half the menus were full of seafood dishes! Remember, I was sensitive to this because Gloria doesn't do seafood. Mark said he never ate much seafood in Italy, especially in people's homes, implying that Italians don't eat seafood.

I don't think Mark would appreciate or understand the fax I sent home shortly after Gloria arrived:

The first week Gloria was here she loved it. Then, one day she says, "I want to go home." HAHAHAHA!! Now, she knows how I felt about the food here after I arrived, and why!! Maybe she is eating only bread and salads for the rest of the trip! We had dinner tonight at a South American restaurant, and it was really a nice change of pace. They had Margaritas, Manhattans, and Irish coffee on the drink menu, unlike Italian restaurants.

. . .

An interesting sidelight of trying to adapt to a culture has to do with how the people handle numbers. How do Italians count?

As I was growing up, for example, my mother would remind me that if I were in Italy I would be one year older! She said when you reach, say, 15 years that you are no longer 15 but rather you are in your 16th year. So, people would say you are 16. I don't know if this is still true or not but I accepted it since it seemed to coincide with the way we count centuries. Besides, mothers just know, right?

How they calculate holidays is interesting, too. When Italians take a week of vacation, it is referred to as the *dieci giorni* (ten days), to include not only the work week but the adjacent weekends, too. To my mind, that's nine days, not ten!

Then there is the quindici *giorni* (fifteen days) which is supposed to signify two full working weeks plus the weekends. But isn't that 16 days?! If you find this baffling, welcome to the club! On the other hand, if you understand it, please feel free to e-mail me at anytime and let me know what I am missing.

Don't forget that if you want to indicate the number "two" with your fingers, you are advised to use thumb and forefinger, not forefinger and middle finger, as we do in the USA. Otherwise, people will think you have to "go potty."

. . .

Numbers or not, you have to be very, very careful with the pronunciation of Italian words. Just a little slip of the tongue and people would think you are cuckoo. For example, consider my *Cazzo-Cozze* experience as I explained it for the readers of *Home and Away* magazine:

Boys Have the Mussels

I was dining at a nice ristorante in Italy and decided to try the mussels. The correct Italian word is cozze, *but I guess my pronunciation sounded more like* cazzo, *which is the word for male genitalia. The waiter smiled and said, "No, signore, I think you want* cozze.*"*

19

WELCOME TO AMERICA

These were the final days. It was time to prepare for the trip back home. The road from Torino to Dayton would be long and arduous. We would be leaving Torino for the last time ten days prior to our actual departure for the States. Ten days more of touring and partying before returning to the good ol' USA.

. . .

Recall that I had spent the first 80 days of my once-in-a-lifetime trip by myself, teaching and sightseeing and eating. Then, for 18 days following Gloria's arrival on my birthday, she and I would enjoy Torino together and take some short trips using the apartamento as a base. Now, for the final 10 days of our journey we would be touring still other parts of Italy after having said *arrivederci* to many good friends and acquaintances in Torino.

We set out to settle expenses and make sure everything in the apartment was in order. We made arrangements to meet with Giuseppina and Rosina a day or two before our exit since our departure would be early in the morning.

The two Italian ladies came to the apartment, returned our deposit, and received our forwarding address. They placed a call to the phone company to get a final reading on the number of "units" that we used and owed for. The cost was surprisingly modest, contrary to what I'd been told about telephone costs in Italy!

Meanwhile, I was wrapping up things at the school, marking exam papers, calculating final grades, turning them in to the office, and saying my goodbyes to the students and staff. Oh, and sending a final fax to the USA to remind the kids that we would soon be home.

> *Looking forward to seeing all of you. We will be home, of course, on Sunday, the 17th. If you want to come over to the house on Monday night, the 18th, anytime after 6:00 will be fine. We will probably have something like baked potatoes with toppings for everybody. You don't have to bring anything but if you do want to bring* hors d'oeuvres *just make sure it is NOT anything Italian — hahaha!!*
> . . .

One of the fun things we did during that final week in Torino was to host a farewell dinner for some friends from the school.

You see, I had this 300,000 Lire (about $200) fee from the Chamber of Commerce seminar that was burning a hole in my pocket. And I was looking for some way to "give it back" before leaving the school. Hosting a nice dinner as a kind of farewell party struck me as a neat idea! So, I talked to Jera about it and she liked the idea, too.

It was a wonderful dinner at a place Jera suggested. There were eight of us: Marelli and his lovely wife, Sylvia, Mark and his lovely bride-to-be, Rafaella, Jera and her talented dog, Aida, my lovely wife Gloria and me. Jera helped us interpret and understand some of the menu items. To the best of my recollection, there was no minestrone on the menu.

By the time we left the restaurant that night, people were likely referring to us as the "Noisy Americans," seeing as we were having such a great time talking and laughing aloud, enjoying each other's company. I remember looking around the dining room at other people who were just sitting there, quiet and deadpan, *troppo serio*, not the happy Italians I expected to find on my journey to the Peninsula. A Sicilian woman I talked with later about this said that it was characteristic of people from Torino. "They are more reserved," she said.

Our Italian, American, and Italian-American friends were not so reserved, however, and it felt good looking around the table, seeing everyone taking pleasure in the dinner party. They were gracious, too, giving Gloria and me farewell mementos of incredibly delicious *Piemontese* chocolates, and an Italian liquore in a bottle shaped like the famous *Torinese* building, the Mole (MOH'-LAY), located in downtown Torino, and said to be the tallest brick structure in Europe. We expressed our appreciation to everyone, drank a toast to good health and good fortune, and knew we would miss our new friends who had helped us so much during the preceding weeks.

We would think about them often in the following days as we toured Florence, Sorrento, Rome, and Milan. We would think about the leaking hot water heater left behind in the apartment! The leak actually occurred a half-hour before the taxi was coming to pick us up!

Picture this. The water heater mounted on the wall above the bathroom sink begins to discharge a steady trickle of water. Now the good news is that most of the water is draining into the sink instead of onto the floor. However, the bad news is that between the water tank and the sink is an electric light fixture. So, we decide to take a plastic trash bag and wrap it around the light fixture, hoping to avert an electrical short and fire. Then we called Giuseppina to tell her what had happened, just in time before our *tassi* arrives to take us on our merry way!

・・・

The 10-day trip proceeded according to plan, for the most part. First, we took the train to Milan where we checked two suitcases at the train station so we could travel light(er). Next, we hopped on a train to Florence where we had booked a hotel for the night. From Florence we traveled to beautiful Sorrento (two nights), Rome (three nights), then back to Florence for three more nights, with our final night in Italy at a palatial old hotel near the Milan airport. We strayed from our original plan that would have given us two nights in Florence and one in Switzerland after realizing that we would be trying to cram too much into an already tight schedule.

When we came through Florence the second time, we were given a special treat. Snow! And lots of it! They say that snowfall in Florence is rare. Well, it snowed quite heavily while we were there. It was beautiful but also cold and wet. And it made it difficult to get around.

We opted for a bus tour that included a trip to Fiesole, one of the hill towns of Tuscany. The driver, obviously not accustomed to the snow, struggled mightily to get the bus up the steep and winding hill, maneuvering through three to four inches of slush. Then, when we arrived at the top of the hill where normally they stop and let people get out and see the view, the driver simply turned the bus around and took us back down the hill! I think he was fearful that conditions were getting worse! Or perhaps he felt an urgent need for a shot of espresso after traversing so much snow!

・・・

Probably the most unique and exclusive hotel we stayed at during the entire trip was a place in Florence called the Brunelleschi, located near the famous cathedral with the famous dome of the same name. This is an interesting part of town. The taxi had to negotiate some very narrow alleyways to get there.

Brunelleschi Hotel is first class. The furnishings and decor are extraordinary. The service is almost impeccable though a little snobbish. The rooms are among the best in Italy, and the bar reminiscent of elegant cocktail lounges of New York City.

We found our room or, more accurately, suite, in an old medieval tower connected to the main part of the hotel, but actually in a different building. After taking an elevator up several floors, and walking some distance down two hallways, we then had to climb a stairwell to a loft-like area that contained several suites.

When we opened the door and walked in, we felt like Alice in Wonderland! The walk-in closet alone was as big as some rooms we'd had in other hotels! The bathroom was elegant—and included a towel warmer, a Jacuzzi, and tons of bright light!

As soon as we had a chance to size-up the place, Gloria asked how much it was costing us. I didn't know, so I called the desk and found out they had given us an upgrade since the hotel was not totally booked. Be that as it may, our price was still more than $300, per night! Expensive, I know, but well worth the once-in–a-lifetime experience!

As much as we enjoyed Florence, the weather was miserable—dreary, cold, and wet. We were both sick by the time we departed for Milan. It was the first time since arriving in Italy that either of us was ailing, as we both came down with a bad cold. I think it was the stress plus changes in the weather, going from mild in Rome and Sorrento, to cold and inclement further north.

. . .

A Travel channel video refers to Milan as "the secret Italian capital known for the three F's—fashion, football, and flirting." Information published by the American Consulate says this:

> *Welcome to Milan. You have arrived in one of Italy's liveliest and most cultured cities, the center of industry and commerce, the closest common point to the Riviera, the Adriatic, the Lakes, and the rich Po Valley plain.*

In Milan we were fortunate to have Mark to show us around. He made a special trip, by train, just to meet us there. I think he has a special affinity for Milan, having gone there often to visit friends and some of his favorite places.

Mark took us to see La Scala (the famous opera house), the Duomo, and the Galleria, all of which are in the same vicinity. We rode the *metropolitana* (subway) to get there from the train station. There were throngs of people everywhere we went.

La Scala is probably the most famous opera house in the world. Although I am not an opera buff myself, I could appreciate the history and fascination of this beautiful hall, the interior of which has been described by some as "elegantly shabby."

Inside, La Scala is stunning, shaped like a big horseshoe with boxes throughout the wraparound balconies, about five levels deep, everything covered in a red damask and trimmed with gilt, illuminated by huge crystal chandeliers. I was told that, as in the old days, people still yell and throw stuff if the performers don't measure up to the high Italian standards. People in the upper balconies like to throw stuff like tomatoes and eggs down onto the peons whose seats are on the floor in the center of the 'U.' There is a similar example of this in the classic movie `Cinema Paradiso` where a certain prominent person who always sits in the balcony spits on those below.

The *Duomo*, the cathedral of Milan that is said to be the last of Italy's great gothic structures, took five centuries to complete! It was begun in the year 1386, but not finished until the 19th Century. That's 500 years later! Maybe they had a few strikes along the way?

The third largest church in the world, this *Duomo* of Milan has an unbelievable cadre of 2,000 statues adorning the spires of the exterior and a seating capacity of 40,000! It is simply breathtaking.

Nearby the famous duomo is the famous Galleria, touted as the very first and most elegant enclosed shopping center in the whole wide world, going back to the late 19th Century. Its formal name is the Galleria Vittorio Emanuele. This is a really neat place! Its steel and glass-covered, cross-shaped arcade occupies about six to eight square blocks, with lots of opportunity for shopping on the way between the Duomo and La Scala.

There was another distinctive feature about the Galleria and I asked Mark to refresh my memory about what it was called.

> *Remember when you took us to the Galleria in Milan, there was a "spot" where people would stand and whirl around for good luck? What was that all about? Was there some kind of emblem on the ground where people would stand?*

I did recall that the emblem, whatever it was, was the symbol of the city of Milan. It was embedded into the sidewalk.

Minestrone/Carusone

Peter,

That was a symbol of a bull on the sidewalk and yes, if one stands on it and whirls around once it is supposed to bring one luck. I have done it many times and look at all the luck I've had. Io sono vivo!

     Mark

 Ha! Mark was making a joke. He was saying look at all the luck I've had—"I am alive." (Io sono vivo!) A little bit of Italian humor there, although sometimes I think Mark is really more Austrian and Montanan than Italian!

     . . .

 Mark took us to a really neat place for lunch, just a small eatery but it left a big impression. We made it a point to return there during our second trip to Italy. It is called *Luini* and is located on a side street just outside the *Galleria.*
 Luini specializes in *panzerotti,* the deep-fried or baked cheese-filled crescent, sometimes filled with meats and other foodstuffs. They tasted so good that I couldn't help but wonder if something like this could become popular in the States.
 Luini's is a small bar-like place with no room to sit and eat inside. Customers mostly buy the panzerotti and take them outside to eat, or stand inside at a counter along the wall. Customers completely filled the space, shoulder to shoulder, back to back, when we were there, and I remember thinking, "Man, they must be making a million bucks here, because this stuff is so popular. And it's so good!"
 I think that a place like Luini would be a big hit in the USA because a panzerotti, if served fresh and hot, is not

only delicious, but convenient to eat. It can be consumed on the run like a fast food. And surely if Americans are interested in anything, well, it has to be quick, easy, and convenient to eat on the run, right?

When it was time to go, we hopped the subway again and were soon back at the train station. After Mark helped us to claim our two pieces of luggage and put them on the airport bus, along with the rest of our stuff, we bid him farewell. He has been a good friend.

. . .

After a short night's rest, our final Italian experience would be to spend a couple of hours waiting at the Malpensa Airport. We were quite favorably impressed with the facility. We had not seen much of it upon our arrival but now had time to poke around. (The Italians have been criticized by the EU for inadequate airport access. You see, there is no rail connection at Malpensa and the highway to Milan is only a two-lane road!)

For such a large airport serving such a large city and surrounding region, Malpensa was relatively calm and quiet. I began to wonder why. Of course, Milan has another airport closer in, Linate, but this is the one that handles most of the international flights from the USA and some other countries.

Compared with airports like LaGuardia in New York, Malpensa was exceptionally quiet. Then we discovered why, that they have a "noise pollution reduction" policy. Aha! Great idea! They do not broadcast public announcements over a loudspeaker system, but rather use signs to instruct people as to where to check monitors for the information they may need. Compare this with New York and other major U.S. airports, where there's a constant barrage of nuisance announcements (not only flight announcements but also obnoxious personal pages). I was quite sensitive to this since we had had a rather long layover at LaGuardia, and I remember thinking that a person can't even read a book there without being bombarded with noise!

Malpensa has a separate play area for children and that really helps keep the noise down, too. It is a spacious, attractively designed area enclosed behind soundproof glass so that parents can keep an eye on their bambini.

. . .

Someday, someone will discover a way to snap his fingers and instantaneously be transported from one continent to another, maybe from one planet to another! I believe that.

Until then, the eight hour trans-Atlantic flight in a tiny cramped seat is a major deterrent to the prospect of frequent international travel. It is for me. The flight is tiring and boring. It is most uncomfortable and unsettling. (This was even before 911 and all the terrorist threats.)

On the top of that, at the time of this trip I was still a smoker! (Okay, so nonsmokers just wouldn't understand.) Thus, I was elated to finally arrive in New York and my first chance in more than eight hours to inhale one. But the good feelings did not last long. The relief at being back home quickly turned sour as the process of going through customs in New York City was like arriving in yet another foreign country.

The rude behavior of U.S. customs agents was a shocker, one that I will never forget! *"This is America?"* I exclaimed. *"We were treated better in Italy!"* Is it not possible to be firm and courteous at the same time? I would advise anyone flying international NOT to come back through New York City. Anyplace else in the country has to be better! Minneapolis, for example, as we would learn on our next trip.

20

WAH, I MISS IT AND WANNA GO BACK!

Travelling is the ruin of all happiness! There's no looking at a building here after seeing Italy.
—Fanny Burney (1752–1840), English author

The Romans had an expression for it, *tempus fugit.* For those of you who took German or Russian, that's Latin for "time flies."

During the time I was there in the Old Country, for those 80 days and 80 nights, time often seemed to pass quite slowly, especially before Gloria arrived. Then, before I knew it, it was gone. Poof! The trip was over, and there I was back home. Back to the normal boring stuff again!

But I was not exactly the same person as when I had left Ohio for Italy. Granted, three-and-a-half months is not a long time, not by the norms of a Tim Parks, a Frances Mayes, or anyone who has spent years abroad. Still, it is a lot longer than the two or three weeks a typical American family might spend on vacation.

Consequently, I became keenly interested in how a person changes as a result of living in a foreign culture. I began reading what expatriates had to say, and started examining my own feelings. Had I really changed? Was my thinking and point of view any different than before? Did I change any of my core values or were they solidified?

When you are "over there" you are not here. And, when you are here, you are no longer over there! This may not make any sense, and yet what I am trying to say is that a part of you—who you are and who you think you are—now belongs to the places and the people you have experienced along the way.

Here is a good example of what I am driving at. These comments were made by the mother of a Massachusetts native living in Milan as she was collecting things to take back to Italy at her daughter's request—things like Ban deodorant and Pepperidge Farm cookies.

> *"Susan's funny," she said. "When she's in Milan, she only wants American things. When she comes here, she wants what's Italian."*

Like Susan, what you may find when you return home is that things are not exactly the same as you remember them. Something has changed. People are different. You are different. In fact, if you have close family and friends waiting for you, it is possible that you have grown somewhat apart, even though you kept in touch during your absence! Because now you have acquired a set of experiences that lacks common ground, experiences that others cannot relate to in the same way that you do.

If you are not careful, you will find yourself unsatisfied no matter where you are! When in Italy, you're whining about the stuff you miss from back home. And when you are back in the USA, alas, you are complaining about what you miss from over there.

> *Those who choose to live in a country different from the one in which they were brought up seem to be in a constant tug-of-war between accepting, discovering, and loving the new country, and missing, honoring, and defending the old one. Not so much because one is better and one is worse, but because our upbringing and culture help form our identity, as do our later adventures in foreign lands.*

These personalized comments are taken from an article entitled *"The Fickleness of Foreigners,"* written by Jessica Halpern and published in *The Informer*. Her discussion focuses on how to balance one's feelings about two different cultures, and how to resolve issues of identity and preference.

> *When people ask... what's it like to live in such a beautiful country? The truth for me is that it has its ups and downs... People want more. So I start going into detail. And what do I find? That I start out with the good stuff—and I think this is because I don't want people to think I'm a fool, choosing to live in such a horrific society where people don't work 'til they're thirty and where restaurants are so stingy that you're lucky to get a piece of lemon with your fish... The people I'm close to will get my opinions on everything good and bad sooner or later, and will know that I'm balanced in my judgment. But if it's a relative stranger at someone's buffet lunch, he or she may end up with the impression that "all I want is what's Italian."*

> *And then I'm back in Italy. And a relative stranger asks me, "Don't you miss America? What's it like there?" And again, I don't want to seem like a fool for coming from a place where kids carry guns in elementary school, or where Wonder Bread is what people use as a mattress for their Marshmallow Fluff. So I say that I miss the independence and creativity of young people, the fact that you can eat at a restaurant at 4:00 in the afternoon if you happen to be hungry, and the way people are always pleasant and helpful in shops. And the stranger may go off grumbling about the chauvinistic American.*

· · ·

When Mark finally moved back to the States, after two years of living in Italy as a newlywed, he brought his Italian bride with him to live in California. That's when I asked him, by E-mail, if he could compare and contrast the two cultures. Here is what he said:

> Peter,
>
> *I miss Italy a lot but San Diego sure is one nice city. I miss the food, the people, the lifestyle, and just about everything about Italy. But I do know that the opportunities are much greater here for Raffaella and me. I can finally think really serious about my career and maybe I can get that Ph.D.*
>
> Mark

That was shortly after Mark and Raffaella made the move. Weeks later, Mark wrote me again, this time after a sobering experience on his way home one night.

> *I came back to school on Friday night and worked until about 10:00 P.M. Then I met Raffaella at work and we had dinner at home. It is so nice to have work so close to home (about 50 yards from the apartment complex), and living in the heart of San Diego is wonderful. The only problem is some of the street people are always asking for money and one night some guy wanted to roll me but I was able to ditch him. One thing about living in Italy though is I never once felt threatened.*

An interesting and candid observation! So, things are not perfect back home, either, despite the inconveniences one may experience abroad.

• • •

Back home I soon realized that not all the weird things I witnessed in Italy were necessarily unique to Italy. There were odd things at home, too! It dawned on me that the reason I happened to notice some of these weird things back home was because now I was filtering from a different perspective.

For example, about a month after our return, I was in a Big Boy restaurant in Dayton, Ohio, a coffee shop much like a Carl's or Denny's–signaling from a distance for the waitress to bring me my bill (*il conto*), by making a writing motion on my hand. But, the waitress thought I meant that I wanted a pen! (Hey, even the Italians are smarter than that!) I felt like I was trying to communicate in another foreign country!

On the Internet, there is a "Gourmet" website that discusses when to eat in Italy and how to eat Italian style. It warns that when entering a restaurant "solo diners may be relegated to poor table locations." Hey, if you think about it, isn't that true here in the States, too? If you are dining alone, first the hostess will say something like, "Just you?"

or "Just one?" Enough to make you feel like crawling under the table… "Yes, it's JUST me!"

Riding my bike around the condominium complex where we live, I noticed all the empty balconies on the apartment buildings nearby. Nobody sitting out on their balcony, even in weather that was pleasant! I recalled how I had made a big deal about the same thing in Italy. Maybe this phenomenon is not unique to the Italians?

Another thought-provoker: Driving by the Colonel Glenn Road ramp off of I-675 on the way to school one day, and noticing piles of unsightly broken glass and trash. If I had seen this in Italy, what would I have thought? Would I be generalizing by saying that Italians don't keep their streets clean? Hmmmm.

• • •

I asked Jera about the bad reputation Italian hospitals have, and was she familiar with this situation firsthand. This is what she told me:

> *This is true all over Italy. There are always stories of these things happening. I have seen the opposite there in that one of my students had an emergency appendectomy there and they saved his life (ruptured appendix).*
>
> *But there are not enough nurses, well-trained or otherwise or technicians. Also, the buildings are old, overcrowded, and dirty inside. Certainly I'd rather be sick in the USA even if you end up paying for it the rest of your life!!!! CIAO—stay well,*
>
> *Jera*

• • •

Something I thought about a lot after returning is how the highways of the *autostrada* serve mainly the intercity traffic flow, not intracity traffic. This is a significant difference in my mind between our cultures. Their expressways begin at the outskirts of one city, take you to the outskirts of other cities. They do not create ribbons of concrete in the middle of the urban areas that tear apart established neighborhoods, divide communities, and separate people like our highways do here in the States. Perhaps, that is why most cities over there have vibrant public transportation systems of trains, subways, buses, and trams.

. . .

I am still enamored of the notion that Italian-Americans may be more Italian than Italians themselves. Recall that we are asserting that Italian cuisine differs from Italian-American cuisine due to the fact that they (the Italians in Italy) have changed. Here is still further evidence.

John Murphy's comment on the subject, in an editorial in *The Informer*, seems to support the Carusone argument! Here are some excerpts from Murphy's article:

> *I've been here over twenty years and am still learning things daily. ...some of the certainties I thought I knew often turn out to be partial truths or totally inapplicable in certain circumstances.*
>
> *...something that I learnt years ago—almost immediately in fact—is that you say buon appetito before starting to eat. You think that still applies? Wrong! ...if you are dining with...people who consider themselves slightly upper-middle class (or higher), then you will generally find that they shun any mention of buon appetito.*
>
> *In fact, in so-called 'good society' it would seem that there are all sorts of things that we have generally picked up from Italian 'riffraff' (middle*

class downwards it would seem, though I confess this is a novelty to me too) which are real no-no's. The classic example is saying salute! (bless you!) when someone sneezes. (Now they) insist that you should not react at all in such circumstances, the logic being that reacting merely highlights the culprit's embarrassment.

Precisely the point I have been trying to make throughout the book. That *they* changed, not us! And, so, you have to decide for yourself. Where is the *real* Italian food to be found, in the dishes and cuisine of us Italian-Americans who are proud preservers of our rich heritage? Or in the stuff they try to pass off as "Italian" in Italy today?

. . .

What will I miss the most? What aspects of life in Italy will I reminisce about in years to come?

When I began writing this book, I wasn't sure of the answer to that question, except for the issue of minestrone soup. Over time, however, the answer has clarified itself. Especially as I have gone through a soul-searching, it has brought home to me the things I wish I could experience once again.

For example, I have already talked about the *briosche* and *cappuccino* for breakfast, especially cappuccino with a flower design on top as served by Charlie in the school bar. Marble floors instead of all this wall-to-wall carpeting that collects bacteria and dirt. The attention to detail. Little things like real cream in the Irish coffee as served by the friendly bartender in the lounge of the Brunelleschi Hotel. The wonderful presentation of food, and the beautiful way things are wrapped and presented to you in the stores, shops, and bakeries. The man operating the street-sweeping vehicle on Via Cercenasco who stopped to pick up a single piece of paper the brushes missed!

I also miss the trains, the buses, the people and their idiosyncrasies, the charming neighborhoods where people walk and talk, the familiar places, and, yes, even the food as an adventurous and delightful experience.

I miss the day-to-day opportunity to engage in meaningful dialogue with people from another culture. A chance to interact, to try out your knowledge of the language, and observe and deal with their responses.

Some other things I miss are the penne pasta at Noe's Pizzaria, always cooked perfectly al dente, the wonderful gelata, the daily challenges of trying to figure out things like the washing machine, Italian drivers, and those frequent but unpredictable strikes. The churches and the architecture. The train stations. The famous places. The surprises. All of these I will remember fondly.

. . .

"Tutto fatto!" I remember well the sound and intonation of her voice when Cristina, one of the candy store ladies responded to my question. Her inflections were delightfully musical. Like many phrases of the Italian language, this one caught my fancy due to its simplicity, harmony, and repetition of the "t" sound. *"Tutto fatto!"*

There will always be a special place in my heart for the "candy store ladies" and their husbands. The assortment of candies in that store around the corner from my apartment was only exceeded by the hospitality of the family who ran the place. That's why I chose to buy a lot of their candy and send it back home.

Walking in one day to ask if they had had success ("s*uccesso?"*) in taking my package of candy to the post office to find out how much the postage would cost, the response was quick and sure. *"Tutto fatto!* ("All done!") I will always remember not only shipping the candy back home and eating a lot of it while there, but touring their *laboratorio* (the back room where they make the candies), and enjoying the hospitality they extended me on every visit to their store. And if, for some reason, I would ever forget the details, I can always pull out the video we recorded of them and watch it again!

. . .

If you are a chocoholic, you will fall in love with Italy. The chocolate candy, especially in the Torino area, is incomparable to anything made in the States. That is the only way I know how to describe it in terms that justify its superior taste and quality.

. . .

Months after our return we had an interesting experience communicating with another candy store in Italy, one that was the source of a gift graciously presented to us the night of the farewell dinner. We tried to order more chocolate candy from this store through the mail!

Marelli's wife, Sylvia, had given us a wonderful assortment of liqueur-filled chocolates that were scrumptious! We took them home and in a matter of weeks they were gone. Since I had sent candy home from Italy when I was there, I thought it would be no problem to have some sent again, so I wrote directly to the candy store in the town of Cuneo where Sylvia had bought our farewell package and asked them to send me more. I enclosed 50,000 lire (about $35) with instructions to take the postage out and send as much candy as the remainder would buy. I wrote the letter in Italian, with the aid of a dictionary, of course.

Weeks and months went by and everyday when I got home I would open the front door to see if there was a package for me from Italy. Everyday the result was the same. Nothing! I was not so much worried about the loss of the 50,000 lire since that was money already spent. I just wanted the candy!

Finally, not ready to concede defeat, I wrote to Jera at the school and explained the situation, suggesting that perhaps Marelli or his wife who lived right there in Cuneo might stop by the candy store and find out what happened to our order.

Marelli to the rescue! I envisioned a startled candy store proprietor who likely thought he'd never hear again from the stupid *Americano* who was dumb enough to put real money in the mail! Haha!!! I guess we fooled him.

> *Dear Peter-*
>
> *Silvia just called as she went to your candy store. They were waiting for someone to contact them as they cannot ship outside the country. Also, it would cost L. 50,000 just to ship a kilo of chocolates!!!!! So she (Sylvia) will get your chocolates and mail them in May when they come to the U.S.*
>
> *Ciao,*
Jera

All ended happily. Sylvia used the 50,000 lire to buy as much candy as she could, then informed me when she and Marelli were coming to the States. A couple of months later she mailed us a package from the East Coast. *"Tutto fatto!"* We finally received the chocolates we were craving, and the postage only cost Sylvia $7.00.

· · ·

Some of the students who took the Italy course from me at Wright State had already been to Italy, most had not, and a few were planning to go, which was a strong motivation for taking the course.

Jim Kremer, for example, and his wife, Janice, were planning just such a trip, which they have since taken and passed along more information back to us. That's how it goes in life, doesn't it? We help them. They help us. What goes around, comes around.

Some of you who are completing this book will make the trip to Italy someday and enjoy many of the same places and things that we did. If it is your first trip abroad, you will need all the help you can get! So, here are eight important tips to help you get started so that your trip will be an enjoyable adventure rather than an international nightmare.

1. Do Your Homework

The first piece of advice is to make the commitment to do your homework before leaving. In other words, prepare, prepare, prepare. Read the travel guides and culture books, highlight key pieces of information that you want to go back to, talk to people who have gone there before, and make lists of things that need to be done before you leave. It would be presumptuous of me to recommend certain books or guides because there are so many good ones out there. However, I can tell you what materials (updated editions noted), in addition to the Internet, I used in the Italy course, namely:

BOOKS:
- *Culture Shock: Italy* by Raymond Flower & Alessandro Falassi, 2003
- *Italian Neighbors* by Tim Parks, 2003
- *That Fine Italian Hand* by Paul Hofmann, 1991
- *Neither Here Nor There: Travels in Europe* by Bill Bryson, 1999
- *Rick Steves' books*, 2005

VIDEOS:
- *Il Postino, 1995*
- *Cinema Paradiso, original version with English subtitles*

2. Plan for the Season

Consider the weather of the season when deciding what time of year to visit Italy. For example, you could avoid some of the fog, rain and wintry cold that we experienced in November and December by going in September or October. However, you may want to avoid July and August, which is when the tourist hordes are heaviest, unless you like crowds and excessive heat. My Aunt Helen says the best time to go is in the spring.

3. Pack Lightly

If you are like most people, you will want to pack just about everything you own, to be sure that if you need something unexpectedly, it will be there. Big mistake!

Don't forget that whatever you pack you will have to carry. There are no porters at the train stations so you'll have to lug all your stuff from platform to platform, up the steep steps of the rail cars and, once inside, lift them up to the overhead rack. Don't count on someone else to help you. Unless you book a tour, of course.

As a rule of thumb, my advice for the men is to pack two or three changes of clothes in addition to what you wear on the plane. You can hand wash underwear and socks every couple of days. If you get desperate, you can always buy something over there to add to your wardrobe and bring it back as a souvenir. Gloria's advice to the women is to take only the clothes on your back, and then buy more when you get there (typical female ploy)!

4. Purchase a Eurailpass in Advance

If you plan to ride the trains, you will want to buy a Eurailpass before leaving the States. They are not available in Europe since they are intended only for tourists, not for the local populace. A travel agent can obtain what you need but you will have to first determine the number of days in each country that you anticipate riding trains.

5. Buy the Foreign Currency You Need

You should buy some foreign currency before leaving the States so that when you arrive, you will have some "spendable" money to see you through the first day or so. Contact your local bank a few weeks before departure. Make sure you have an ATM card that will work over there (not easy to determine, for sure, but ask around), in addition to a major credit card like VISA. Above all, don't forget to leave your wallet at home!

6. Learn a Little of the Language

I believe it is of paramount importance to learn some of the language. Do it! Even if it is only 10 or 20 words, learn some Italian before you go. It is rude not to! You are imposing on others to decipher your language and many people may rightfully get impatient with you. How do you think we earned the right to be called Ugly American?

You can find some basic primers at any good bookstore, some with audio cassette or CD so you can hear the pronunciation. Even the travel books have sections with basic "tourist" vocabulary. Or, better yet, for the more adventurous, take a five- or ten-week continuing education course in the Italian language. Oh, and don't forget to study Noe's menu at the end of this book to give you an advance warning of what you can expect to encounter in the restaurants.

7. Get Ready for Some Crazy Driving

If you plan to drive a car in Europe, inquire at AAA about an international driver's license. Plan to be patient with the crazy driving of the Italians. As my friend, Jim, so aptly put it, "They are taught that their job is to close the space between you and the next car." This is unlike the advice we are given here in the USA of leaving so many car lengths in between. So, don't be surprised to have other cars on your bumper, even at high speeds.

8. Do an Attitude Check

Finally, on the topic of mental preparation, it is important to relax and have an open mind. Richard Hill, author of *We Europeans*, says it very well:

> *Before making judgments about other peoples' ways of thinking and living, try to understand why they are the way they are. Learn to listen (learning the basics of their language is a start), travel to the real places and not just the tourist spots, mingle, talk, and live with these other Europeans, seize any opportunity to work with them, absorb all the impressions you can, try to understand their culture and, at the end of it all, still keep an open mind.*
>
> . . .

The cold and snow in Dayton were a grim contrast to the Italian environment of the past three-and-one-half months. There I was, shoveling piles of white stuff in the courtyard of our cozy condo, barely a week after enjoying the warm sunshine of Rome and Sorrento. Home at last!

EPILOGUE

About the Book

It started as a joke. I said "Mark, I don't understand any of this, especially the food. I'm going to write a book about it when I get back." It was intended to be just a wee bit tongue in cheek, not to be insulting. However, judging from Mark and Rafaella's reaction to the draft, I suspect that some might be offended. After all, there are those who look very seriously at everything, and especially when they think something is a slur on all Italians!

Well, I have always been extremely proud of my Italian heritage, and I guess I feel that since I am Italian it gives me the right to joke and tease about Italian stuff if I want to. I do not see it as disrespectful or trying to insult anyone. But, rather to help people lighten up a bit, to laugh together about our little idiosyncrasies (we all have them), and not be so thin-skinned about everything.

How neat it would be to be able to talk with my grandpa again and ask what he remembered about these things. What was it really like when he left Italy more than 70 years ago? Where in Bellona was the house they lived in? Did I come close to it when I was there? Did I see it? How much have things changed since the 1920s? And last, but not least, would *he* think Italy has the *real* Italian food today?

I think about the power of being able to laugh at oneself. *Non fare troppo serio, signore!* (Don't be so serious, sir!) I think if all races and nationalities were able to joke and laugh, good-naturedly, about some of each other's traits, we would all be a lot closer to one another, a lot more understanding, and there wouldn't be so many anti-defamation lawsuits, either.

When I was a boy, I was always one of the smallest kids in my class. When Sister lined us up to go to church, or lunch, or recess, it was from shortest to tallest. Other boys sometimes picked on me because I was so small, thinking I would be a good target. Sometimes they even called me ethnic names, or names like kerosene and macaroni. If I snitched to the teacher, or otherwise made a big deal out of it, things would quickly get worse! But, if I refused to show that the teasing and taunting bothered me, if I made light of it, or slugged them back and then walked away with my head high, that took all the fun out of it for the bullies, and they soon stopped picking on me. The moral of the story is *non fare troppo serio, signore!*

. . .

A Note about My Second Trip

Three years after this Italian-American's first trip to Italy, we headed back across the Atlantic. There were four of us: Gloria and I, her sister Marcie, and their friend, Sandra. After spending two days in Amsterdam, we headed for Milan where I attended an International Retail Conference on Lake Maggiore.

During the remainder of the three-week sojourn, we managed to visit Milan, Torino, Florence, Rome, Venice, and Verona. Upon our return, Mark and some others were just so eager to pop the question.

"Was the food better this time?"

APPENDIX
Noe's Menu

PIZZE

PARIGINA - Olio-Formaggio-Prosciutto Crudo	10.000
FOCACCIA - Olio	5.000
MARINARA - Olio-Pomodoro-Aglio	5.500
MARGHERITA - Olio-Pomodoro-Formaggio	6.000
NAPOLI- Olio-Pomodoro-Formaggio-Acciughe	6.500
FUNGHI - Olio-Momodoro-Formaggio-Funghi	7.000
PROSCIUTTO - Olio-Pomodoro-Formaggio-Prosciutto Cotto	7.000
PROSCIUTTO E FUNGHI - Olio-Pomodoro-Formaggio-Prosciutto e Funghi	7.500
4 STAGIONI - Olio-Pomodoro-Formaggio-Prosciutto-Carciofi-Funchi-Olive	8.500
CAPRICCIOSA - Olio-Pomodoro-Formaggio-Prosciutto-Carcofi-Funghi	8.000
4 FORMAGGI - Olio-Pomodoro-Formaggio-Gorgonzolo-Fontino-Parmig.	9.000
OLIVE - Olio-Pomodoro-Formaggio-Olive	6.500
BISMARK - Olio-Pomodoro-Formaggio-Prosciutto Cotto-Vodo	8.000
CIPOLLA - Olio-Pomodoro-Formaggio-Cipolle	6.500
SALAMINO PICCANTE - Olio-Pomodoro-Formaggio-Salamino Picc.	8.500
GORGONZOLA - Olio-Pomodoro-Formaggio-Gorgonzolo	8.500
GORGONZOLA E SALAMINO - Olio-Pomodoro-Formaggio-Gorgo.-Solom.	9.500
4 FORMAGGI E SALAMINO - Olio-Pomodoro-Formaggio-Fontin-Gorgo.-S.	11.000
WURSTEL - Olio-Pomodoro-Formaggio-Wurstel	7.000
PROSCIUTTO CRUDO - Olio-Pomodoro-Formaggio-Prosciutto Crudo	10.000
NOE - Olio-Pomodoro-Formaggio-Prosciutto-Funghi-Cipollo	8.000
GORGONZOLA E CIPOLLA - Olio-Pomodoro-Formaggio-Gorgo-Cipollo	9.000
ALLE VERDURE - Olio-Pomodoro-Formaggio-Melansone-Peperoni-Lucch.	10.000
CERTOSINO - Olio-Pomodoro-Formaggio-Certosino-Rucola	9.000
RUSTICA - Olio-Pomodoro-Formaggio-Prosciutto Crudo-Rucola	10.500
ALBESE - Olio-Pomodoro-Formaggio- Carugoll'albese	12.000
SALCICCIA - Olio-Pomodoro-Formaggio-Salciccia	9.000
FRUTTI DI MARE - Olio-Pomodoro-Formaggio-Frutti de Mare	12.000
CALZONE - Olio-Pomodoro-Formaggio-Prosciutto Funghi-Carciofi	9.000
Rinforzo supplemento di	1.000

Aggiunto di Origano o Peperoncino a richiesta

ANTIPASTI

Antipasti della Casa	S.Q..
Affettato Misto	10.000
Prosciutto Crudo	9.000
Prosciutto di Cinghiale	15.000
carne all'Albese	10.000
Caprese	8.000
Insalata di Mare	18.000
Cocktail di Gamberetti	18.000
Cozze alla Marinara	10.000

PRIMI PIATTI

Spaghetti a Pomodoro	7.000
Spaghetti alla Carbonara	9.000
Spaghetti al pesto	8.000
Penne all'Arrabbiata	8.000
Penne al Salmone	18.000
Spaghetti Alle Vongole	10.000
Spaghetti Alle Cozze	9.000
Spaghetti Agli Scampi	15.000
Spaghetti Al Gambero	15.000
Agnolotti Alla Piemontese	9.000
Agnolotti in Salsa Noci	9.000
Tagliatelle a Mo do Nostro	9.000
Tagliatelle al Salmone	12.000
Tortellini Panna e Prosciutto	8.000
Risotto Alla Parmigiana	8.000
Risotto Ai Formaggi	10.000
Risotto Alla Pescatora	12.000
Gnocchi Alla Bava - Al Pesto - Ai Formaggi	10.000

SECONDI PIATTI

Bistecca Ai Ferri	15.000
Paittard ai Ferri	10.000
Milanese	8.000
Valdostana	10.000
Roast beef	9.000
Scaloppine a piacera	10.000
Gamberoni alla Griglia	20.000
Scampi alla Griglia	20.000
Orate alla Griglio	18.000
Branzino all Griglia	18.000
Feittura Calamari e Gamberi	18.000
Pesce spada o Palombo alla Griglia	18.000
Zuppa di Pesce su Prenotazione	25.000

CONTORNI

Insalata Verde	4.000
Insalata Mista	5.000
Insalata Pomodori	5.000
Patatine Fritte	4.000
Spinaci al burro	5.000
Formaggi Misti	4.000
Grana	5.000

Minestrone/Carusone

DESSERT

Dolei Del Carrello	5.000
Macedonia di Frutta	4.000
Fragole con Gelato	5.000
Affogato al Caffe	5.000
Affogato ai Lipuori	7.000
Caffe'	2.000
Caffe' Corretto	2.500
Whisky	5.000
Coperto	2.000

BEVANDE

Birro piccolo chiava Gosser alla Spina	3.500
Birra Media " " "	5.000
Birra piccolo rosse Farsons alla Spina	4.000
Birra media " " " "	6.000
Birra Bott.. Leffe 33 CI.	6.000
Birra Bott.. Ceres 33 CI.	6.000
Birra Bott. Adel Scott 33 CI.	6.000
Birra Bott. Bonne-Esperance 75 CI.	12.000
Birra Bott. Chimav 75 CI.	12.000
Coca Cola piccola alla spina	3.000
Coca Cola media alla spina	4.000
Bibite in Lattina	3.500
Vino cortese alla Spina ½ L.	5.000
Vino Coretse alla Spina 1 L.	10.000
Barbera del Monferrato Bott.	10.000
Dolcetto di Orada Bott.	10.000
Souvignon della Torre Bott.	13.000
Fontana Candida Bott.	12.000
Rosato Chiaretto Bardolino Bott.	12.000
Acqua Minerale ½ L.	1.500

Peter S. Carusone is Professor Emeritus of Marketing at Wright State University. While researching *Minestrone*, he was Visiting Professor at the University of Torino in Italy. He has since taught courses and given talks on Cross Cultural Consumer Behavior. He has also taught in other foreign cultures, such as France and California. Dr. Carusone and his wife, Gloria, reside in Dayton, Ohio.